OSSA OSTENSA

OSSA OSTENSA

A PROVEN SYSTEM FOR DEMYSTIFYING LATIN

BOOK ONE

Laura Pooley

THE CATHOLIC EDUCATION PRESS
Washington, D.C.

The paper used in this publication meets the
requirements of American National Standards for
Information Science—Permanence of Paper
for Printed Library Materials,
ANSI Z39.48-1992.
∞

ISBN 978-1-949822-08-3

DEDICATION

IN MEMORIAM REGINALDI

(November 14, 1939–December 25, 2020)

sate magistro meo qui postea mei oblitus in melius tamen vitam convertit meam, ac nihilo minus usque sequentium vitas, desiderioque meo, cuius communicandae Latinitatis ratio durior quamvis ludus aliorum sidera restinguit. huius durat mihi lumen (licet non eadem sit mens neque aetas), praebentibus se comites et defunctis et adhuc me sublevantibus illis: esto venturis adiumento tironibus sicut ratio mihi illa unice valuit, libelle.

Sprung from my teacher, who though later forgetful of me nevertheless changed my life for the better and continually likewise the lives of those coming after, and from the one I miss, whose method of sharing Latin, although a rather hard training school, puts out the stars of other men. Whose light endures for me (although my mind is not the same nor my age), as long as those people are offering themselves as companions, both those who have died and those who are still supporting me; little book, be a source of help for the recruits to come, just as that method has been uniquely influential in my case.

CONTENTS

REFERENCE MATERIALS

FOREWORD

BY DANIEL MCCARTHY, OSB

Introduction

Any instructor could be at a loss for knowing where to begin teaching the Latin language using the method developed by Reginaldus Foster. How did Reginald present his teaching in the classroom? Can other teachers do the same? The answer is emphatically yes and the workbooks of this series are proof. Reginald and I encourage this in our introduction to the volume *Ossa Latinitatis Sola: The Mere Bones of Latin:*

> freedom is left and also the responsibility is left to the individual using this book [*Ossa*] to personalize it to their own spontaneous way of presenting the different parts of the Latin language.[1]

Laura Pooley has achieved this. She teaches in these workbooks in the same way Reginald taught her. Her version springs from an entire year learning directly from Reginald himself. Laura was one of the notable students who attended the sessions of all five Experiences of Latin in the course of one academic year at the Gregorian University in Rome. That experience has been distilled through her more than twenty years of teaching Latin and is now available in the workbooks of this series. She is well aware of the range of texts and textbooks used in universities and schools, so she knows what works and what does not! She has also had reference to the draft and now published volume

Daniel McCarthy, OSB, is a monk of Atchison, Kansas; Pontifical Institute of Liturgy, Sant'Anselmo, Rome; Liturgy Institute London; and KU Leuven.

1. Reginald Foster and Daniel P. McCarthy, *Ossa Latinitatis Sola: The Mere Bones of Latin* (Washington, D.C.: The Catholic University of America Press, 2016), xxxii.

Ossa this past decade and the subsequent volumes of *Latinitatis Corpus* while she has been teaching at the Benedictine Institute, Ealing, London, in addition to other teaching commitments. These have confirmed her personal experience of learning from Reginald himself, as distilled through her decades of teaching, because his method is very coherent and solid, and it works.

Reginald is hailed as a genius by some writers, who then conclude that other people are not able to use his method to good effect. While he may have been singularly gifted, Reginald's method is imitable, learnable. Laura has integrated his method into her teaching and developed in her own right his way of presenting the Latin language. The burden rests not on the genius of the instructor but on the method of approaching authentic Latin literature, which itself will teach anyone who applies both curiosity and perseverance. The goal is not genius excelling, but clear and patient understanding of a human expression originally conceived and expressed in Latin.

The full presentation of Reginald's teaching in *Ossa* might give the wrong impression that his classroom encounters were spent presenting this teaching. Rather, *Ossa* is intended as background reading to prepare for classroom work and for later rereading, while Reginald spent most of his time in the classroom helping students to understand a variety of Latin authors.

In Reggie's Classroom

Reginald usually began each classroom encounter by writing a full Latin sentence on the board and helping the students to understand it. Next, they used it to form their own Latin expression based on this authentic thought. He chose the sentence not only as a review of previous material, but as an introduction to the material to be presented later that session. In a way he helped students realize what they do not yet understand but are soon to learn. After working with one or more initial sentences to get going, he then would hand out the *ludus domesticus*, one of his famous domestic games, never called "homework." He always seemed to know which student to ask about any given answer so that he might emphasize his point. He did not belabor the *ludus*, because he had already corrected each one of them in several colors with his famous markers.

Reginald preferred to leave the presentation of the new teaching to just a few minutes even at the end of the session, so that most of the hour-and-a-half together was spent reading Latin texts. At some point during each session the students would turn to their copies of the reading sheets and begin the process of coming to understand a different author each time, and Reginald was careful always to read authors from different eras, genres, contents. The texts themselves illustrated the teaching of that day, and in this way Latin literature is the primary teacher. If more time was needed on any one point, Reginald knew that it was better to help the students understand the thought expressed in Latin rather than to rush on to the next topic.

I attended several summer sessions in Rome and soon realized a pattern. Throughout the first of two months Reginald resisted giving the teaching on the sequence of tenses. Rather, he would regularly present challenging texts so that participants would come to see that their previous understanding of the sequence was not adequate to the literature. He resisted their rising demand for his teaching until the fourth Saturday afternoon, when he would take about five minutes and "on two thumb-nails" he would sketch the sequence of tenses. The relief was palpable and followed by a desire to read more literature to see this teaching at work. This is the model: (1) use literature to develop an awareness of the need to learn, (2) limit the teaching to one element, (3) return to the literature.

An awareness of the need to learn develops when the instructor presents literature that is well beyond the students' abilities and then elicits what the students already know and develops it a bit further, while the teacher provides the rest of the sentence. What the students know is then seen in its natural context as part of a complete thought yet to be fully understood. From the beginning students are working with the full language while learning a bit at a time how it functions, with the teacher serving as the guide. This process of guided learning resists the easy satisfaction students receive when studying only sentences that lie within their ability to understand. The difference lies in the ability to arouse curiosity, to confront limited understandings, to see greater connections, to stretch beyond the limits of what has been taught so that students may develop their questions and seek greater answers.

Essential Teaching

Reading each encounter in the *Ossa* is a good preparation for Laura's classroom experiences, or "lessons," so that time together may be dedicated to reading literature and giving a distilled presentation of Reginald's teaching. Those distilled teachings are one major component of this series. Laura helps the teacher to use Reginald's method by indicating the essential elements to be presented during the classroom encounter. By keeping these presentations to their essence, there is more time for reading Latin texts together so that literature may be the guide. Laura helps instructors know what explanations to give and how to begin to teach using Reginald's method.

Choosing Texts and Readings

The next difficulty is selecting texts for classroom use. Reggie and I place great confidence in teachers of the Latin language, when we leave

> the choice of concrete texts and examples up to the teacher personally, as some will prefer examples of Latin uses from the poets or prose, from classic authors, from medieval authors, from the Renaissance, from church Latin, from any source.... and the examples will be discovered and used by the individual.[2]

Laura Pooley has greatly simplified this process for Latin instructors. She uses materials presented by Reggie in the year she spent with him, and supplements them with her own materials, drawing examples from authors of every era of Latinity. This series shows teachers how they can compile their own examples from Latin literature so that this freedom and responsibility to personalize the presentation of the Latin language may grow within instructors as they listen and respond to their students' struggles and as they continue their own encounter with the Latin language by reading and incorporating new materials from authors of every age.

For each of the 105 encounters presented in our first volume, *Ossa Latinitatis Sola*, Laura presents examples from genuine Latin literature that illustrate the material being studied. Laura does not alter

2. Foster and McCarthy, *Ossa*, xxxii.

the original Latin texts in any way, so that the learner must confront real Latin literature on its own terms. For example, she does not rearrange the word order of the Latin sentence so that an English speaker would recognize the meaning of the sentence just from the word order, thereby delaying the necessary task of recognizing the function a word plays in a sentence from its ending. This is essential if one is ever to enter into the process of discovering the meaning of a Latin sentence in its unfolding. Rather, Laura helps the learner to approach and gradually understand each Latin text on its own terms and from the very first encounter. Students may bring their own texts for the other participants to consider together. Laura has responded abundantly to our encouragement "not to limit ourselves to one author, but to open up the whole Latin world to every learner."[3]

Laura Pooley has generously provided texts from both classical Latin literature, which is taken up once again in the Renaissance, and from church Latin, which continues throughout the medieval era, so that the teacher and student may choose to use either exclusively classical or only ecclesiastical Latin literature and still have an abundance of illustrations of the point at hand. Or they may choose to combine the texts and thereby approach the full body of Latin literature of every age, author, and type. Some of the texts selected are brief, and can be used to begin the session or as a quick guide for learning. Other texts are considerably longer and represent almost a packet of reading sheets of the type presented in *Ossa*. The difference is that in *Ossa* numerous reading sheets are presented as a full packet of original Latin literature given at length, whereas here even the longer passages are chosen as illustrations of the teaching presented in their encounter. This will help ease the instructor into the process of eventually making a full set of reading sheets every year so that the instructor may also find challenges in reading fresh Latin literature.

When one of our teachers was at the last minute unavailable to teach the Third Experience of Latin, I was able to use the second volume of this series without difficulty. The distilled presentations of the teaching in this volume helped me to focus my presentations in class. Even the experienced teacher will find beneficial the abundance of both short and long Latin texts to use each day.

3. Reginald Foster and Daniel P. McCarthy, *Ossium Carnae Multae: The Bones' Meats Abundant* (Washington, D.C.: The Catholic University of America Press, 2021), lii.

Conclusion

Laura Pooley is to be commended for producing this complementary series for teaching the Latin language. Teachers who are hesitant to use the method developed by Reginald Foster will find a helpful introduction here. Experienced educators will find a colleague's helpful contribution. Independent students will find further resources needed for learning on their own.

A TEACHER'S PROLOGUE

BY JONATHAN DAY

As codified in sources like Escoffier's *Guide Culinaire*, French methods for making the "great" dishes and sauces called for hard-to-find ingredients (a pig's foot, for example, to add unctuousness); they distinguished three kinds of skimming: *écumage* (removing scum); *dégraissage* (removing fat); and *dépouillement* (creating a "skin" of impurity, in order to subsequently remove it). The "greats" required days of tedious work, once done by unpaid apprentices: simmering, scumming, skimming and skinning, degreasing, straining, sieving, reducing. When everything was done correctly, the results were astonishing, but the methods so painstaking that today they have been abandoned or greatly simplified, even in top restaurants.

On the other hand, radical shortcuts—stirring cornstarch and vermouth into a can of supermarket bouillon and calling it a sauce—deliver mediocre results. As in so many areas of life, it is tough to simplify the classic methods without first having mastered them.

When I first encountered *Ossa Latinitatis Sola: ad Mentem Reginaldi Rationemque*, by Reginald Foster, OCD, and Daniel McCarthy, OSB, I wondered if I could ever use it. The sprawling title gives it away: this book spans 831 pages and weighs in at 4 pounds (1.8 kg), even in paperback. It contains pages and pages of untranslated Latin and some English that is almost as difficult to read. And yet the *Ossa*—one of five of the late Reginald Foster's works in print or in preparation—is a treasure, because it presents his innovative and highly effective system for teaching the Latin language. His methods—I can testify to this both as a student and as a teacher—really work; they leave the learner with a deep and lasting understanding not just of the superficial meaning of a Latin passage, but also of its "bones"—its inner workings, what some linguists would call its deep structure.

The authors say that the *Ossa* can be used for self-study or reading on the beach. Not so, unless the reader is an experienced Latinist or has a skilled tutor. Even for Latin teachers, the book on its own presents formidable difficulties: for example, finding appropriate reading passages at every stage. In a year-long introductory course in the Foster method that started in September, the ablative case [function] would not appear until something like April. Yet all of the reading passages are to be drawn from Roman authors, unadulterated, who were not sparing in their employment of ablatives, subjunctives, and gerunds. The very first "reading sheet" for the "first experience" is from Horace's epistolary poems. No small steps for little feet here.

What is more, the magic of Foster's system relies heavily on his *ludi domestici*, ingeniously crafted homework sheets that prod and cajole the student into doing things with Latin that she never would have thought possible. Foster wrote these anew for each class he taught, burning each year's set afterward, so that he—and teachers who used his system—would be forced to create new ones. Fortunately, his disciples have collected large sets of the *ludi*, which someday will be published. Unfortunately, that publication is still a long way off.

Laura Pooley, a classicist who has thoroughly mastered Reginald Foster's methods, has come to the rescue with this set of books. I have used the first volume in teaching introductory Latin in an intense two-week summer course at Ealing Abbey, near London. The volume was a pleasure to work with, even in an earlier draft form: Laura presents the essentials of the method in a few swift strokes. She provides judiciously chosen reading passages, a good selection of *ludi domestici* for students and teachers to work through, and neatly worded tips at every stage:

> "There is no understanding of Latin without building up a base of vocabulary, and the best way to learn it is to read and look up words again and again."
>
> "Always translate the *-que* as if it was on the front of the word it is attached to: apples pears*que* = apples and pears."
>
> "It can be time consuming to realize that you are looking at a PP3 stem, and work out which verb it is.... This is a lifetime's work, but the best possible way to become independent and fluent in the language."

Throughout the summer course, I and my students had to work hard; Laura's is hardly a paint-by-numbers approach. But the effort paid off: after two weeks of intensive work, my beginners could read *and understand* this passage from Caesar's *Civil War*:

omnes, qui sunt eius ordinis, a Pompeio evocantur. laudat promptos Pompeius atque in posterum tempus confirmat, segniores castigat atque incitat. multi undique ex veteribus Pompei exercitibus spe praemiorum atque ordinum evocantur, multi ex duabus legionibus, quae sunt traditae a Caesare, arcessuntur. conpletur urbs et ipsum comitium tribunis, centurionibus, evocatis. omnes amici consulum, necessarii Pompei atque ii, qui veteres inimicitias cum Caesare gerebant, in senatum coguntur. quorum vocibus et concursu terrentur infirmiores, dubii confirmantur.

I have written more extensively elsewhere about Foster's method;[1] here, I will sketch a few of its innovations that I think make it so effective. All of these are reflected in Laura's books.

1. All of the readings—classical, post-classical, modern ecclesiastical—are "real Latin"; there are very few made-up sentences. The learner encounters the language in its pure form, gaining confidence from the start.
2. The noun and adjective cases are presented as "functions" rather than new grammatical labels—subject, object, "of-possession" (genitive), etc.—skipping several mental steps on the road to understanding.
3. The student, from the start, produces Latin sentences—"prose composition" begins almost on day 1—but builds these on the Roman authors, especially Cicero, by transforming their sentences.
4. Similarly, the grammatical paradigms are learned not by parroting tables, but by mastering transformations: singular into plural, active into passive, present into future.
5. The call for "smooth English translation," so often heard from Latin teachers, is here subordinated to a demand for renderings that fully expose the inner workings of a Latin sentence.

This last point deserves some expansion. It took me a while to work out how the *Ossa* could unashamedly present such English "translations" as

1. "On Reginald Foster's Latin," *PrayTell*, at https://www.praytellblog.com/index.php/2021/01/03/on-reginald-fosters-latin.

For the more valuable the entire common good is than the consulship or the praetorship, the former ought to be administered by all the greater care than these latter things ought to be sought. (Sallust, *Iugurtha* 85)

Or

To some people it seems that only they sin against the Holy Spirit who, washed with the bath of regeneration in the church, and—the Holy Spirit having been received as such as a great gift of the savior—afterwards they, ungrateful, have sunken themselves in some death-bringing sin. (Augustine, *Enarrationes in Psalmos* 71)

Eventually I realized that the objective was not "translation" but a sort of "unpacking"; akin to but not identical to the French *explication de texte*. I now think of the broken English that pervades the *Ossa* and occasionally turns up in Laura's work as "Reggie code." Its great advantage is that, with the Reggie code in hand, you can turn a passage into heroic couplets, rap lyrics, or blank verse, all of it "true to the Latin." Yet without the code, there is no real understanding, only guesswork. Like the *mirepoix* vegetables that are meticulously chopped at the start of making a great sauce yet discarded as intermediate products long before a dish reaches the table, the unpacking is of the essence to any fine translation.

There is still more work to do in making Reginald Foster's powerful insights more widely available. As just one example, teachers need to be able to adapt and transform the material, without laborious retyping. That will require electronic distribution, and clever legal and technological work to ensure that authors are compensated for their labor, even while material achieves the fluidity and adaptability that electronic presentation requires. This may seem a "modern" idea—encouraging imitation, adaptation, and re-presentation—but in fact it is thoroughly "classical." After all, a "classic" is a work that perpetually rewards rereading and rethinking, that has unlimited depth.

Laura Pooley's work is an important step in that direction. Her approach is not identical to Reginald Foster's, but she follows firmly on the tracks that he set out. Her books will be an invaluable aid to teachers at all levels.

London, January 2020

ACKNOWLEDGMENTS

Anyone who has worked with Reggie or attended his classes will recognize the enormous debt I owe to him for many of these materials and the expression of his teaching ideas. As I write, in January 2021, we are mourning his departure from this world. He has left a giant-sized hole. I hope that the inclusion of many of his actual words and materials will contribute to the perpetuation and dissemination of his spirit and ideas. I take full responsibility for any mistakes or departures.

I'd like to thank my colleagues at the Benedictine Institute in London, where these books were conceived, who have supported their progress: Fr. Daniel P. McCarthy, OSB, Fr. James Leachman, OSB, Jonathan Day, Daniel Vowles, and Clare Cogswell. Also my student there, Tym Marsh, and all my students over the years. My thanks also to Dr. Charles Weiss for sharing resources and answering random questions, and for the scrupulous remarks and painstaking attention of Anne Needham and all those at CUA Press.

OSSA OSTENSA

INTRODUCTION AND HOW TO USE THIS BOOK

princeps Aeolium carmen ad Italos / deduxisse modos

Horace, *Odes* 3.30

"You will not apply my precept," he said, shaking his head. "How often have I said to you that when you have eliminated the impossible, whatever remains, however improbable, must be the truth?"

Arthur Conan Doyle, *The Sign of Four*, "Sherlock Holmes Gives a Demonstration"

Our ancient masters knew about the evolution of language—like Horace, above, or Propertius bringing Italian mysteries through Greek dances and so forth. My hope is that my slim volumes will create a *locus* where the traditional methods of Latin instruction may intersect with the innovations of Reginald Foster, OCD, and provide a practical course from which all types of learner may benefit. One thing is certain: Latin is Latin. All courses are indisputably trying to communicate one language. This is my attempt to bring everything I have to bear upon that task, to make Latin as accessible as possible, as living as possible, as understood as possible. If that means trying on it new suits, new gestures, well, our models were the ancients. What the ancients never did, though, was to betray the integrity and essence of the original. Their *imitatio* brought the original home.

Reginald's Pedagogy and Instructions

I was taught by Reggie for one academic year in Rome. By that time, I had completed Latin A Level (the final exams in British schools), and further papers, with top grades, and had done two years at Oxford (seven years of Latin in total, with great teachers and modern textbooks). And yet, I could not read Latin with any accuracy or fluency. I got things wrong and guessed too much. It was going to interfere with my finals. Action needed to be taken. And so I went to Rome and did, simultaneously, all of Reggie's Experiences that taught the grammar (First, Third, and Fourth). I went to the Second Experience, where we (well, Reggie mostly) chatted in Latin for over an hour. I did up to six *ludi domestici* ("home games" or homework assignments) a week. The result was that I stopped guessing and became quite good. I smashed my finals. I learnt incalculably more in seven months than in all of the previous seven years. That *wasn't* to do with Reggie's well-documented charisma, intoxicating though it was. It *was* aided by the fact that I had no choice but to improve within a short timeframe and *had* learned, after seven years, to be a pretty good student (read: attention, application, effort). But Latin became clear to me primarily because the methodology used (and devised) by Reggie was unbelievably clear, accurate, and efficient. There was nowhere to hide and everything to play for. I am eternally grateful to Reggie. I also know from my exposure to students over nearly two decades that my experience of learning Latin for years, but never really grasping it, is very common indeed. My purpose in this course is to make the revelatory experience I had with Reggie in Rome available to as many people as possible, like passing on a set of golden keys.

Although in his book *Ossa Latinitatis Sola*, Reggie has deliberately avoided producing anything that could be a "class manual to teach Latin," he clearly does want teachers to try out the method. Reggie adjures teachers to see introducing the language as a series of "personal encounters rather than mechanical calculations."[1] This should involve finding "different authors each year so that the encounter with the Latin language may remain fresh and challenging." From the entire corpus, he leaves "the choice of concrete texts and examples up to the

1. Reginald Foster and Daniel P. McCarthy, *Ossa Latinitatis Sola: The Mere Bones of Latin* (Washington, D.C.: The Catholic University of America Press, 2016), 24.

teacher personally";[2] these texts should be just unadulterated extracts from various Latin authors. He wanted the practice element, the *ludi domestici*, where the students exercise their knowledge independently, to be composed by teachers themselves.

For me this leaves a gap between the expectation and the practical reality, especially where teachers have not had any personal experience of Reggie's teaching, or where someone is trying to learn independently, without even the benefit of a teacher's presence. It is extremely difficult—or if not difficult, then time consuming—for any teacher, let alone an independent learner, and, heaven forbid, a beginner, spontaneously to fillet out a clear example of, say, the future perfect tense from an uninterrupted wall of Cicero, or Jerome, or Horace. But this lacuna is the result of idealism and impracticality, rather than ideologically unsound foundations. It leaves the methodology open to criticisms such as these expressed in Paul Gwyne's review of the *Ossa*, that the *Ossa* is monolithic and doomed to be dust-gathering.[3] The reviewer goes as far as saying:

> I do not know of any high school teacher who has successfully implemented Foster's 'method' *in toto*. It would be a very brave teacher indeed who ditched the Oxford, Cambridge, Advanced Placement or Baccalaureate examination boards in favour of Foster's method. Universities should be more flexible...[4]

As usual, the criticism is reserved principally for the method and its difference from traditional methods, and not for the world that ignores and side-lines it. The last phrase, in fact, might imply exactly that: "universities should be more flexible...." Yes, they should, as should schools and exam boards. But actually educators do reach for many innovations in an attempt to save Latin: using books with interactive links to games to be played on an *iPad*; trimming the syllabus and requirements so that Latin remains "accessible"; accepting people with no Latin into university courses, teaching them traditionally and too fast, and then watching half of them drop out. That whole thing can do a disservice both to the language and to the students. Everyone is losing out, while the educational institutions try to look modern.

2. Foster and McCarthy, *Ossa*, 32.

3. Gwyne, review of *Ossa Latinitatis Sola*, by Reginald Foster, *Bryn Mawr Classical Review*, August 2018, available at https://bmcr.brynmawr.edu/2018/2018.08.31.

4. Ibid.

As an answer to the challenge the *Ossa* presents to teachers, this workbook will try to demonstrate a course that could provide an alternative way for those who want to keep the communication of Latin meaningful. I am a teacher. I have taught students privately. I have taught primary school students. I have taught secondary school students. I have taught the so-called "gifted and talented" and I have taught those who needed learning support. I have taught those with dyslexia. I have taught those for whom English is a second language. I have taught those from private schools. I have taught those from state schools. I have taught at Nottingham and Oxford and Cambridge Universities. I have taught adult learners, from PhD students to seminarians to mothers and retired enthusiasts. I am a teacher, and my only objective is to pass on what I know as clearly as I can, as sympathetically as I can, as kindly as I can. My only interest is in the students' outcomes, in helping them to learn and just feel better, to know more. I am happy to say that my students have had grand success. And I have only ever used one method—*Reggie's.*

However, I wanted to take away at least one of the obstacles and criticisms and say: here you are, you can do it, I've done it. This is my version of Reggie's teaching, what I've taken away as being most helpful for my students and for their outcomes. Anything in it can be manipulated. In my view, the grammatical terminology, the *vocabula rerum*, is incidental. The shortness of the "concordance" (reference sheet 1) will demonstrate how simply and quickly one could flip back to traditional terminology. Equally, the order in which you teach things is not set in stone. My lessons are in an order slightly different from that in the *Ossa*. One year you try one thing, another the next. It doesn't matter what you take as examples, classical, post-classical, poetry, prose. I want this course to be, as it were, a consolation and a beacon. I've made it shorter, so that each level will come separately, and so that you can turn the pages. I've tried to explain an aspect of the language using as few words as possible. I've tried to demonstrate and translate the language at work. I've tried to give short and accessible practice from real Latin from all periods. These books, this course, are just *examples* of how the method can look in the classroom. It's not perfect. A teacher's work is never finished. But at least it's there. *The end is where we start from.*

It is easy to criticize teachers and teaching systems, and the deafness to Reggie's system is part of that. In the spirit of positivity and collaboration, I invite the reader to experience that this way of seeing the language has many virtues and spectacular clarity, and that, in the interests of learning and being able to read Cicero, or Vergil, or Jerome, or Heloise, students will benefit from opening themselves to the method. People can fall away in the attempt and start criticizing. I believe that this is because this work is not only radical, but it requires a sustained effort on the part of both students and teachers. It is painstaking, slow, detailed. It requires you to think and to work things out on your own. But the results, when the students commit themselves and toil and labor, are spectacular.

The Spoken Latin Controversy

There's a new fashion in the world of Latin, which means that not only Reggie's ways, but also traditional translation methods based on grammatic paradigms, come under fire. Suddenly everyone's speaking Latin. I'm delighted by this, if it works for you. All Latin is good. Personally, I can speak Latin, if a bit slowly, and I can understand what is said to me, likewise slowly. The reason I'm not amazingly proficient is that my main focus in understanding Latin has been to read the works that have been handed down in Latin. If speaking the language helps me to understand a text better, then I'll add it as one learning tool among others. But, a bit like the *iPad* games or language apps, I feel that, for Latin, it's both a bit of a carrot and a red herring. It might lure me in, and I may make fast progress at first, but the wall of Cicero or Lucan may well be as impenetrable as ever.

I want to get into that wall, the nooks and crannies, the cement, the pointing, the shape of the bricks; I'm not interested in telling you what I did yesterday. My carrot for those who lust to articulate themselves in Latin is a great deal of thinly disguised "prose composition" (not just a sop to the traditionalists). When you have read a short piece of wonderful Latin, be it Seneca or Heloise or Petrarch, it is a great idea for practicing and consolidating to adapt that Latin. It was a key feature of Reggie's classes that he would ask students to switch the person doing the verb, or switch the tense, or reverse the form that had been read from singular to plural or vice versa, or flip a sentence from active into passive, and give the new Latin. Surely, anyone can see how quick and nimble one's use of Latin would become by this method, how *fluent* one would become with the vocabulary, forms, and endings. For the purposes of this course, this will be our version of, or contribution to facility of, spoken Latin. As often as, after your questions and translation, you are asked, "Say in Latin . . ." this is precisely what you are practicing, and it is a small step from there to saying whatever comes into your head, if you want to, with accuracy and tested style. I will not be addressing the vexed topic of pronunciation in this volume. There are as many ways of saying Latin as countries in the world. If I slip in here and there that a vowel may be long in quantity, it is only in case that makes a grammatical fact more understandable or memorable. "You say tomato; I say tomato. Let's call the whole thing off."

How to Use Each Workbook

All of these materials for teaching and learning come directly from my experience in Reggie's classroom supplemented, with no differentiation, by my own materials. The "workbooks" evolved out of collating my own teaching materials for use at the Latin summer school at the Benedictine Institute in Ealing, London. There, three levels of Latin are offered—beginners, intermediate, and advanced, which roughly equate to Reggie's First, Third, and Fourth Experiences. Essentially, therefore, each workbook contains an academic year's work. The summer school conveys each level's information in ten days, which, unsurprisingly, has been described as a "dump" of information. In fact, you can go as fast or as slowly as you can take something in meaningfully. No one can learn a language in two, four, or six weeks. At the end of the day, there are no short cuts. That is common sense. However, if you have only a short space of time to be taught, you can take away from an intensive course the fundaments, but you will need to work on them and consolidate the material over the following months.

You don't need any equipment for this course except something to write or type on, your brain (on full power) and a dictionary. The best book-format dictionaries for beginners are either *An Elementary Latin Dictionary*, by C. T. Lewis, or *Cassell's Latin Dictionary*, by D. P. Simpson. The best online dictionaries are the Perseus Project Word Study Tools or "Latinitium Dictionary."[5]

5. http://www.perseus.tufts.edu/hopper/search?redirect=true; and https://www.latinitium.com/latin-dictionaries.

New aspects of the language will be introduced in small, assimilable chunks, lesson by lesson. Each lesson is accompanied by translated examples of the language in practice, each area of language is explored through translation practice from either the classical or post-classical era, with vocabulary and prompts or teaching questions, and there is a *ludus domesticus* (a "game" to do independently) after every three or four lessons.

The course does not attempt to say everything there is to say about each item of language introduced. There are plenty of grammar books in the world for this purpose, all wonderful, all true. On my shelves, I have *Latin Grammar*, by Gildersleeve and Lodge; *A New Latin Syntax*, by E. C. Woodcock; Kennedy's *Revised Latin Primer*; and now, of course, Foster's *Ossa Latinitatis Sola*. What I intend to include, in each lesson here, is the essence of a language item, presented in the fewest words possible, in the clearest format possible, which does include (*pace* Reggie!) a few tables. My summary, then, of an aspect of language is my still-imperfect refinement of what I have been teaching students on the ground for years. It's my interpretation of what they *need* as opposed to all I could possibly find to tell them. What is clear, also after years on the ground, is that the search for a "definitive" explanation is a doomed one, as no two human beings will ever receive words or process them in the same way. The language as presented here is as close as I can get, for today, to as clear as possible, for as many people as possible, and should enable all students to go away with a pretty clear idea of how an aspect of the language works and how to apply it immediately to any Latin they are trying to read. For a fuller explanation, you can turn to a corresponding chapter in the *Ossa*, which is why I provide the corresponding chapter number in the contents page.

It should go without saying, but I'll say it once anyway, that the object of every piece of Latin, either following a lesson or as part of a *ludus*, is to understand it: that is, to translate it accurately into your own language. I will not repeat every time, "now translate the passage." The best students will be tripping over themselves to want to know what the sections of Latin mean, anyway. However, translating real Latin is sometimes more easily said than done, and will seem an intimidating business, especially for those setting out as beginners. That is one of the reasons why this method can seem more "difficult" than other textbooks, because it refuses to use the false, confected Latin that is the curse of many courses and, shockingly, public exams. However, using real Latin teaches real Latin much more successfully, so students are asked to make a commitment of time and effort, patience, and faith. Yet, given that it's demanding, you'd be amazed (or not, if you're a teacher), how rarely students help themselves. Therefore, *prior to attempting a translation*, students should take note of the vocabulary given and work systematically through the prompts or teaching questions, and remember those answers, when putting it together. The absolute key here is to *obey the Latin*. Guesswork is outlawed. Follow the steps as per Sherlock Holmes's demonstration and you will come out with something pretty accurate. We want to know what the Latin says—not what you think it says or want it to say.

Translation is another vexed topic. Whilst often adapting original Latin beyond recognition or putting out texts that are not Latin at all, public exams often award points for "style" in translations, or for rendering a passage into "good English." I'd like to advise the complete opposite. I will be presenting original, undoctored Latin. The goal is a translation that is comprehensible and correct in English, but that mirrors the Latin as closely as possible. What you want is to experience Latin internally, which means reading and understanding the Latin, seeing, hearing, tasting, what the author intended you to, not transmuting it into something other. As soon as you write something down you inevitably create a version, which is not really the objective here. So think about rendering the Latin faithfully. For this reason, instances of "rough" or "unidiomatic" English in this volume are entirely deliberate and designed to improve the learner's *Latin*. This should not ever mean pursuing the literal *ad absurdum* or to the point of destroying the spirit of the original. Other people's volumes can address the topic of translation. This book is only about Latin.

The vexed question of how to translate is linked to the vexed question of terminology. What I am seeking is cleaned-out language on both fronts. I want our use of language, whether that of a teaching instruction or a translation, to be the clearest possible to convey what the Latin means. For me, *third-person plural nominative* is less clear than saying *they are the subject of the verb*. Terminology *per se* imposes a layer of interpretation that delays access to the language. Likewise, I'd prefer an ablative absolute rendered rather literally, *the windows having been broken, the boys ran away*, than *the boys ran away with the windows broken*. This is a *bête noire* of mine, the use of "with" for ablative absolutes, which generally creates nonsensical English, but which is more accepted in exam scripts, while the use of the literal "having been," which has the virtue of being accurate, is penalized as bad style.

For those new to Reggie's terminology I provide a concordance in reference sheet 1, which, as mentioned, is actually incredibly simple and incredibly short. The "names of things" is not what any argument should be about. I regularly flip back and forth between old and new, depending on the needs of those whom I am teaching. These new descriptors can be illuminating, and I would encourage comparing my explanation of a piece of language with Reggie's or with that found any other book. I am confident that, despite the relative brevity of each lesson, little of key importance has been omitted and that readers will not find incongruities across the various systems. It is but one language. Latin is Latin. We just need to find a way together of reading it well.

I've divided the translation practice after each lesson into either classical or post-classical authors. You do not need to heed this division or choose one or the other. All Latin is good to read and practice on, and what you read matters not at all. However, I am aware that people are learning for all different reasons and coming from all different backgrounds. A group of classicists from Oxford may not want to read canon law, and a student of medieval theology may be put off by Plautus. Ultimately I'm hoping that you would aspire to be a scholar of all, but I don't want any students to be alienated or put off, so take your pick.

How many of the translations you attempt after each lesson depends on how fast you are needing to get through the material. In any scenario, the course should provide hours of fun and enough material for students to go back time and again.

When finally rendering whole sentences into the vernacular, you need to be aware that there is no word for *the* or *a* or *an* in Latin. Any translator needs to supply these articles to their version, and sometimes you can even throw in a radical *his* or *her* or any such possessive adjective, as you feel appropriate.

Sometimes you may feel that you are being asked questions to which you haven't yet been taught the answer. Sometimes that's good for you, and you should have a go anyway. The information will quickly be coming up, and the required stretch of your mind will be deliberate on my part.

I am a teacher, but I am not interested in my teaching; I'm interested in your learning. If this presentation and practice of the language helps you, that's wonderful. If you prefer something else, that's fine. I offer you one among many voices, a "personal encounter," my current *imitatio*.

LESSON 1

THE NATURE OF LATIN

Two Principles of Word Order

i. Endings

The meaning of most modern languages depends on the order of the words. Compare: "he had stopped a driver" and "he had a driver stopped," or "Marcus calls Maria" and "Maria calls Marcus."

Latin, however, is an *inflected* language, which means the *endings*, rather than the order, of the words change. One tiny change of a letter or syllable can change the entire meaning of a word. The ending of the word will indicate its exact function in the sentence. For nouns and adjectives, it will reveal which one of seven functions it performs, and whether it is singular or plural. For verbs, it will reveal who is doing the action and when it is happening. It is our joy to learn the function of the endings.

For this reason, the order of the words in Latin is not fixed. Word order does not give the meaning—the endings of the words produce the meaning. This produces a tremendous freedom to craft beautiful, architectural sentences.

Look at the following four sentences:

1. **Marcus vocat Mariam.**
2. **Marcum vocat Maria.**
3. **Marcum Maria vocat.**
4. **vocat Marcum Maria.**

In sentence 1, Maria is the object. Her name follows the verb, and the word order happens to reflect the subject-verb-object pattern of typical English.

In sentence 2, Maria is the subject. Latin enables you to finish a sentence with the subject—which demonstrates how trying to translate by starting with the first word can confuse the translator and do violence to the Latin.

Sentences 2, 3, and 4 all mean exactly the same thing, yet the word order is different each time.

ii. Dictionary Forms

Latin is further challenging because the same endings occur all over the place, such as *-is* and *-os* and *-as*, not always with the same significance. The function of the ending will depend on how the word appears in the dictionary. Knowledge of how the words appear in a good dictionary is absolutely crucial.

Use the dictionary to investigate these sentences:

omnis civis gratis donis suis gaudet nimis.

audis patris miris modis omnis vocis.

Translations:

omnis civis gratis donis suis gaudet nimis.
Every citizen is rejoicing freely and very much over his own gifts.

audis patris miris modis omnis vocis.
You hear all the words of the father in wonderful ways.

You must come away from the first lesson with three key principles:

i. Know your vocabulary as it appears in the dictionary. If you don't know it, look it up!
ii. Read the entire sentence; never start with the first word.
iii. Train your Latin eye to analyze the endings.

Classical Latin Reading Example—with Translation

PUBLIUS VERGILIUS MARO (70–19 ANTE CHRISTUM [AC])

torva leaena lupum sequitur, lupus ipse capellam,
florentem cytisum sequitur lasciva capella,
te Corydon, o Alexi: trahit sua quemque voluptas.
aspice, aratra iugo referunt suspensa iuvenci,
et sol crescentis decedens duplicat umbras;
me tamen urit amor: quis enim modus adsit amori?

Ecloga 2.63–68

Vocabulary: *sequitur*: he/she/it pursues/ goes after
florentem: flowering (object)
cytisus, -i (common gender [c]): a shrubby kind of clover

First, use the dictionary and common sense to try to get a sense of what is going on in the passage above. There is no understanding of Latin without building up a base of vocabulary, and the best way to learn it is to read and look up words again and again.

Now use the translation provided below to label in each Latin phrase the position of the subject, object, and verb, and note which adjectives go with which nouns.

> *Translation: The fierce lioness pursues the wolf, the wolf itself the she-goat, the frisky she-goat pursues the flowering clover, Corydon pursues you, O Alexis: their own desire draws each one. Look, the young bullocks are carrying back the ploughs hung from the yoke, and the departing sun doubles the lengthening shadows; but love burns me: for what limit may there be to love?*

Signs of Person in Verbs

Hour by hour, or week by week, the different endings for different word types will be gradually unfolded. Learning Latin is incremental and detailed, so it is best to take small steps and master each new ending through reading and practice, rather than by trying to memorize large chunks of abstract tabulated information all at once.

First word-endings to learn: the sign of the person doing the verb (active indicative) —"person endings"

	Singular (Sing) *Subject Pronoun*	*Verb Ending*	*Plural (Pl)* *Subject Pronoun*	*Verb Ending*
First Person	I **ego**	**-o -m** or **-i**	we **nos**	**-mus**
Second Person	you **tu**	**-s** or **-sti****	you (y'all) **vos**	**-tis** or **-stis****
Third Person	he, she, it **is, ea, id**	**-t**	they **ei/ii, eae, ea**	**-nt** or **-erunt****

** "Time 4 specials"—these endings, *-sti*, *-stis*, or *-erunt*, are used for the **perfect tense only**. The double asterisk in the text (**) will indicate when to use the T.4 special endings. The different possible times of verbs will be covered in Lesson 7.

You can always tell who is doing the verb by looking at the *ending*. The pronoun for that person is therefore never necessary, but can be included for emphasis.

Quick Reading Examples

feci
I did

fecisti
you did

fecerunt
they did

amo
I love

amamus
we love

amat
he/she/it loves

delebam
I was destroying

delebitis
you will destroy

TRANSLATION TIPS

- Read the whole sentence.
- Try to identify the verb first and who is doing the verb. Never start with the first word!

Classical Latin Translation Practice

Titus Maccius Plautus (254–184 AC)

**Nisi quid mi opis di dant, disperii, neque unde auxilium expetam habeo.
itaque petulantia mea me animi miseram habet.
quae in tergum meum ne veniant, male formído ...**

Cistellaria 671–673

Vocabulary: *quid* (object): something
mi (form of the dative *mihi*): to me
opis: of help

1. Which person is doing the following verbs: *dant, disperii, expetam, habeo, habet, veniant, formido*?

Translation: Unless the gods give something of help to me, I have perished, nor do I have from where I might seek help. Therefore my pertness makes me miserable in spirit. I am terribly afraid that these things may come upon my back.

2. By picking out the necessary words from Plautus's verses and changing the person endings on the verbs, say in Latin: "Unless we give something of help, you [pl **T.4 special ending] have died. Therefore you [pl] do not have from where you [pl] might seek help."

Post-Classical Latin Translation Practice

Alcuinus Eboracensis (730–804 Post Christum [PC])

Sis felix semper!

Carmina 248 Ad quemdam episcopum

1. This line means, "May you always be happy!" Say in Latin: "May she always be happy!" and "May I always be happy!"

Biblia Vulgata, Hieronymus [Jerome] (347–420 PC)

Nam, et si ambulavero in medio umbrae mortis, non timebo mala, quoniam tu mecum es.... Parasti in conspectu meo mensam, adversus eos qui tribulant me; impinguasti in oleo caput meum; et calix meus redundat.

Psalmus 22 (23).4–5

1. Which person is doing the following verbs: *ambulavero, timebo, es, parasti, tribulant, impinguasti, redundat*?

2. Reverse (change singular to plural, or vice versa): *parasti, tribulant, impinguasti, redundat.*

3. Can you spot an unnecessary pronoun?

LESSON 2

BLOCK 1 NOUNS (SUBJECT AND OBJECT FUNCTION); NEUTER SUPER RULES

The first set of nouns to learn are grouped in Block 1. Forty percent of all Latin nouns belong to Block 1. Words belonging to Block 1 all have the same endings, which change according to what function the word has in the sentence, what gender it is, and whether it is singular or plural. You can identify whether a noun belongs to this family by how it appears in the dictionary:

1	*2*	*3*	*4*
lupus	-i	**masculine (m)**	a wolf
capella	-ae	**feminine (f)**	a shegoat
aratrum	-i	**neuter (n)**	a plough

For almost all nouns in the Latin language, the dictionary entry gives you four pieces of information:

1. the ending when the noun is the subject and is singular;
2. the sign of which block the noun belongs to, which is also the "of-possession" (genitive) function ending of the noun [*aratri* means "of a plough"];
3. the grammatical gender of the noun (masculine, feminine, or neuter);
4. the meaning of the noun.

Nouns that appear in the dictionary like the three shown above change their endings in the following way:

	M	F	N
subject singular	**-us**	**-a**	**-um**
subject plural	**-i**	**-ae**	**-a**
object singular	**-um**	**-am**	**-um**
object plural	**-os**	**-as**	**-a**

Grammar Notes

- The *subject* is the person or thing doing the verb, the "actor" of the verb.
- The *object* is the person or thing receiving the direct action of an active verb.

Neuter Super Rules

These rules apply to all neuters with (almost) no exceptions:

NEUTER RULES

i. the subject and object ending (singular/plural) for neuters is the same.
ii. the neuter plural subject and object ending is *-a*.

You must know how the word you are reading appears in the dictionary. For now, when you see a noun in the dictionary, and the **second part** is *-i* or *-ae*, then that noun belongs to Block 1.

Lots of the endings look the same.

- A neuter noun ending in *-a* is plural, but a feminine noun ending in *-a* is always singular.
- A masculine noun ending in *-um* is the direct object, but a neuter noun ending in *-um* could be the subject as well.
- Some endings can have more than one possibility: the *-i* ending for masculine nouns, and the *-ae* ending for feminine, can be either subject plural or "of-possession" (genitive) singular.

Ambiguities in Action

lucra prudentia fecit.

Vocabulary: *fecit*: he/she/it produced

- Both *lucra* and *prudentia* look like feminine singular nouns functioning as the subject, or neuter plural nouns functioning as the subject or object.
- Read the whole sentence. Do not start translating with the first word or guessing!
- Find the verb and work out which person is doing the verb: *fecit* (he/she/it). Therefore, the subject of this verb must be a singular word.
- Look up the nouns in the dictionary to check their block and gender. You find *lucrum -i* (n): profit, gain; and *prudentia -ae* (f): prudence. Therefore, *prudentia* must be functioning as the singular subject, and *lucra* as the plural object.
- Make your translation.

nostrum institutum aurum fecit.

Vocabulary: *nostrum*: our

Here, both *institutum* and *aurum* are neuter singular nouns. As neuter nouns, they look the same when functioning as the subject or object. This produces the unanswerable question: did *our institution produce gold*, or did *gold produce our institution*?

Classical Latin Translation Practice

Marcus Tullius Cicero (106–43 AC)

habes causam opinionis meae. (*Ad Atticum* 10.17.4)

Vocabulary: *habes*: [present tense verb]
opinionis meae: of my opinion

1. ______________________________

____

video difficile esse consilium. (*Ad Atticum* 11.15.1)

Vocabulary: *video*: [present tense verb]
difficile: difficult
esse: to be

2. ______________________________

____

litteras cras habebis. (*Ad Atticum* 12.15)

Vocabulary: *habebis*: [future tense verb]

3. ______________________________

____

misi tibi Torquatum. (*Ad Atticum* 13.5.1)

Vocabulary: *misi*: [simple past tense verb (*mitto*)]
tibi: to you
Torquatus -i (m): Torquatus

4. ______________________________

____

sed complere paginam volui. (*Ad Atticum* 13.34)

Vocabulary: *complere*: to fill
volui: [simple past tense verb (*volo*)]

5. ______________________________

____

legi epistulam. (*Ad Atticum* 13.46.2)

Vocabulary: *legi*: [simple past tense verb]

6. ______________________________

____

tument negotia. (*Ad Atticum* 14.4.1)

Vocabulary: *tumere*: to swell, multiply, reach breaking point
[present tense verb]

7. ______________________________

____

reginam odi. (*Ad Atticum* 15.15.2)

Vocabulary: *odi*: [present tense verb]

8. ______________________________

____

Bruto tuae litterae gratae erant. (*Ad Atticum* 16.2.3)

Vocabulary: *Bruto*: to Brutus
tuae: your
gratae: welcome
erant: they were

9. ______________________________

____

iam iamque video bellum. (*Ad Atticum* 16.9)

10. ______________________________

____

equum et mulum <u>Brundisi</u> tibi <u>reliqui</u>. (*Ad Familiares* 16.9.3)

Vocabulary: *Brundisi*: at Brundisium
reliqui: [simple past tense verb (*relinquo*)]

11. ______________________________

____

Adapt Cicero's sentences to write in Latin:

1. They have the causes of my opinion.

____

2. We see the plans.

____

3. You [plural] will have a letter tomorrow.

____

4. You [singular **] sent letters.

____

5. We wanted to fill pages.

____

6. You [plural**] read the letters.

7. The business is reaching breaking point.

8. We hate queens.

9. The horse was welcome to Brutus.

10. He sees wars.

11. They [**] left horses and mules.

Post-Classical Latin Translation Practice

Codex Iuris Canonici 1983

Magna cum diligentia officia adimpleant. (209.2)

Vocabulary: *magna cum diligentia*: with great diligence
adimpleant: [verb in the subjunctive mood (*adimpleo*)]

1. ______________________________

____

Soli clerici obtinere possunt officia. (274.1)

Vocabulary: *obtinere*: to obtain
possunt: [present tense verb (*possum*)]

2. ______________________________

____

Matrimonium facit partium consensus inter personas. (1057)

Vocabulary: *facit*: [present tense verb (*facio*)]
partium: of the parties
consensus (singular subject): consent
inter: between (used with the object ending [+ object])

3. ______________________________

____

si paroecia proprium habeat coemeterium, in eo tumulandi sunt defuncti. (1180)

Vocabulary: *proprium*: its own
habeat: [verb in the subjunctive mood (habeo)]
eo: it
tumulandus: needing to be buried
sunt: [present tense verb (*sum*)]
defunctus -i (m): a dead person

4. ______________________________

Sacras reliquias vendere nefas est. (1190)

Vocabulary: *vendere*: to sell
nefas: an absolute wrong
est: [present tense verb (*sum*)]

5. ______________________________

potest ad causas pias . . . bona relinquere. (1299.1)

Vocabulary: *potest*: [present tense verb (*possum*)]
ad: to (+ object ending)
relinquere: to leave

6. ______________________________

Adapt the canons to write in Latin:

1. We should fulfill the office.

2. I am able to obtain the office.

3. Matrimony makes consent.

4. You [pl] persons make matrimonies but [*sed*] not necessarily [*necessario*] consent.

5. Parishes should have cemeteries.

6. You [pl] are able to leave a possession to a pious cause.

LESSON 3

PRONOUNS; WAYS TO SAY "AND"

Person Pronouns in the Subject and Object

Person		*Subject*	*Object*
First Person	I / me	**ego**	**me**
	we / us	**nos**	**nos**
Second Person	you	**tu**	**te**
	you plural (y'all)	**vos**	**vos**
Third Person	he / she / it him / her / it	**is / ea / id**	**eum / eam / id**
	they / them	**ei** or **ii / eae / ea**	**eos / eas /ea**

You never need the subject form of the pronoun in Latin (why not?), though it can be used for emphasis.

Where there is ambiguity, for example between *vos* being subject or object, or *ea* being feminine singular or neuter plural, you can solve the problem by looking at the verb. In the phrase *ea ea legit*, you might think there is a typo, but *ea* does appear multiple times in the list above. If I analyze the verb, I see it has a singular subject, so one *ea* must mean "she" and the other one "them" or "the things": "she reads them." In the phrase *vos laudo*, *vos* could be subject or object. But when I focus on the verb I see its subject is "I," meaning that *vos* must be the object: "I praise you."

Notice that there are similarities between the pronoun endings and Block 1 endings: *eos—lupos* (masculine object plural); *eam—capellam* (feminine object singular); and the neuter rules apply to pronouns, too!

Quick Reading Examples

ego Romanus sum, tu Graecus es.

I am Roman, you are Greek.

ave Caesar, morituri te salutant.

Hail, Caesar, they who are about to die salute you.

Carnufex, non ego te novi? (Plautus, *Amphitruo* 518)

Villain, don't I know you?

Pyrrhus fertur dixisse: "tu grandes elige, ego, eos fortes reddam." (Frontinus, *Strategemata* 4.1.3)

Pyrrhus is reported to have said: "You choose big men, I shall send them back brave."

Three Ways of Saying "And" in Latin

1. **Et.** The word *et* means "and" and is used to join two equal things not especially closely related. *Et* may also be translated to mean "even" or "also":

   linguam Latinam intellegit et capella!

   Even the she-goat understands Latin!

2. **Ac / Atque.** The word *ac*, also written *atque*, means "and" and is used to join things in closer relationship. *Atque* is not to be confused with *atqui*, which means "but" or "however." One little letter in Latin will kill you!

   pater atque filius Romae habitabant.

   The father and son used to live in Rome.

3. **-que.** The suffix *-que* is used very frequently to join almost anything! It is attached to the end of the second of two things being joined, usually to the first word of the second concept, if the whole thought comprises more than one word.

   Always translate the *-que* as if it was on the *front* of the word it is attached to: apples pears*que* = apples and pears

   SPQR = *Senatus PopulusQue Romanus*

   The Roman Senate and People
   (Here *-que* is joining two words, *senatus* and *populus.*)

   hodie tu studes crasque ego scribam

   Today you are studying and tomorrow I shall write.
   (Here the *–que* is joining two sentences. It doesn't join the specific word *cras* to anything, it connects two sentences, and *cras* happens to be the first word of the second sentence.)

4. **NB:** Both *et* … *et* … and *-que* … *-que* … are used to mean "both … and …"

   et capellae et lupi linguam Latinam intellegunt!

   Both she-goats and wolves understand Latin!

Classical Latin Translation Practice

Publius Ovidius Naso (43 AC–17/18 PC)

Quid cessas currum pompamque parare triumphis?

Epistulae ex Ponto 3.4.95

Vocabulary: *quid?*: why?
cessare: to hesitate [present tense]
triumphis: for triumphs

1. What does the suffix *-que* mean in Latin? Where do you translate it, in relation to the word it is joined to? Which two words does it join here?

2. Say in Latin: "Why does he hesitate, and you [pl] hesitate and they [those women] hesitate?" Express all pronouns, three different verb forms, and use different ways of saying "and."

TITUS MACCIUS PLAUTUS (254–184 AC)

{Antipho} Num quis hic est alienus nostris dictis auceps auribus?
{Philumena} Nullus praeter nosque teque.

Stichus 103

Vocabulary: *praeter* [preposition + object]: except

Antipho says: "Is there some stranger here, an eavesdropper to our words with his ears?"

1. What does Philumena reply?

---

sed videone ego Pamphilippum cum fratre Epignomo? atque is est.

Stichus 582

Vocabulary: *ne*: makes a sentence into a question
cum fratre Epignomo: with his brother Epignomus

---

1. Explain how you can tell who is doing the main verb *video* [present tense], just from the ending on the verb? Say in Latin, expressing all pronouns: "we se," "they see," "you [pl] see."

---

2. If *Pamphilippum* is the object of the verb, what is the subject form of his name?

---

3. Which two pronouns are not strictly necessary in Plautus's line?

---

tu condicionem hanc accipe, ausculta mihi,
atque eam desponde mi.

Aulularia 238

Vocabulary: *condicionem*: [object form of *condicio*]
hanc: this
accipe: accept! [imperative]
ausculta mihi: listen to me!
desponde: betroth, pledge!
mi = *mihi*

1. What is the function of *tu* in this sentence?

---

2. What is the translation of *eam*?

---

3. How else could Plautus have expressed that *atque*?

---

4. Say in Latin: "Betroth him to me!"

Post-Classical Latin Translation Practice

Biblia Vulgata, Hieronymus (347–420 PC)

Et adiuvabit eos Dominus, et liberabit eos; et eruet eos a peccatoribus, et salvabit eos, quia speraverunt in eo.

Psalmus 36.40

Vocabulary: *adiuvare*: to help
eruere: to rescue
a peccatoribus: from sinners
quia: because
sperare: to hope
in eo: in him

1. What does the phrase *et . . . et . . .* mean?

2. All the verbs are future, except for *speraverunt*, which is in the simple past tense. Give a translation of each verb.

3. Use the sentence to say in Latin: "We will help him, and you [pl] will help her; and they will rescue it from sinners, and we will save you all."

Adhuc doctrinam quasi prophetiam effundam, et relinquam eam quaerentibus sapientiam, et non desinam . . . in aevum sanctum.

Ecclesiasticus 24.46

Vocabulary: *doctrina -ae* (f): teaching
quasi: just like, as if
prophetia -ae (f): prophecy
effundam, relinquam, desinam: [translate as future or subjunctive]
quaerentibus: to people seeking
sapientia -ae (f): wisdom

1. From the vocabulary given, *doctrinam*, *prophetiam*, and *sapientiam* must function as what in the sentence? Give the reverse (singular to plural, or vice versa) of those words.

2. Which person is doing the verbs *effundam*, *relinquam*, and *desinam*? How do you write that pronoun in Latin?

3. What function does the word *eam* perform? Give the subject form of that word. What noun is it replacing, and therefore how should it be translated here?

4. What Latin problem is demonstrated by all those words ending in *-am*? What are the three key principles for untangling such knots?

5. Keeping the word order you see in the Vulgate passage given above, write in Latin:

"Still they may pour out words [*verbum -i* (n)] and wonders [*miraculum –i* (n)], and [express the "and" in three different ways] they [express using masculine and feminine pronouns] may not leave us nor [*nec*] you [pl], him nor her, me nor you [sing]."

LUDUS 1

AFTER LESSONS 1–3

Topics covered: *the nature of Latin; signs of persons in verbs and their pronouns; Block 1 nouns in subject and object; neuter rules; three ways of saying* and.

Our Latin learning this year is inaugurated by the Father of Latinity: Marcus Tullius Cicero [106–43 AC], who in the middle of the month of October, 45 AC wrote to his friend Valerius some complete Latin sentences which you can appreciate and use now.

A.

Gratissimum igitur mihi feceris, si Volaterranos omnibus rebus integros incolumisque esse volueris ... (*Ad Familiares* 8.4)

1. Using your Latin eye, identify the two Latin verbs in this sentence whose endings show who is doing the verb.

2. Who is the subject of (person doing) those verbs? Is that subject singular or plural?

3. What is the reverse (singular to plural, or vice versa) of those verb forms?

4. Now give the *they*, *we*, and *she* forms.

The sentence means, keeping the Latin word order:

> "A most-pleasing thing therefore to me you will have done, if the Volaterrans with all things complete and unharmed to exist you will have wanted."

Keep the same Latin word order, but modify the verbs and write in Latin:

5. "Today he will have done a most pleasing thing to me, if quickly and courageously he will have wanted the Volaterrans to be complete with all things and unharmed." [Find "today," "quickly," and "courageously" in the dictionary.]

6. "Soon I will have done a most pleasing thing everywhere, if I will have wanted children [*puer, pueri* (m)] and teachers [*magister, magistri* (m)] to exist always complete with all things and unharmed." [Find "soon," "everywhere," and "always" in the dictionary.]

7. How would the translation change if Cicero had started his sentence *feceris igitur gratissimum mihi*? Explain your answer briefly but fully.

B.

Hanc actionem meam C. Caesar primo suo consulatu lege agraria comprobavit agrumque Volaterranum et oppidum omni periculo in perpetuum liberavit. (*Ad Familiares* 8.4)

1. Your future Latin training will teach you that the subject of this sentence is "C. Caesar." Which two verbs connect to this subject?

2. Give the *we* and *you* [sing and pl **T.4 special] forms.

The second sentence means the following (according to the position of the Latin words):

"This action of mine Gaius Caesar in his first consulship by the agrarian law approved and the field of the Volaterrans and the town from all danger forever freed."

3. What principle of Latin enabled Cicero to begin the sentence with the object, follow with subject and with verb, then another object, and at the end the final verb?

4. If we want to read this passage as Valerius would have, what part of each word do we need to concentrate on as we read each of Cicero's words?

5. Keep Cicero's words and word order, and using his sentence, say in Latin:

"Because [quod] this action of mine by the agrarian law yesterday you [**] approved, immediately we freed the town from all danger forever."

Even after only your third encounter you can understand and use some full verses of Rome's greatest epic Augustan poet—Publius Vergilius Maro (70–19 AC).

C.

The god Mercury is sent down to earth to scold Aeneas for delaying in Africa and building the city of Carthage with Queen Dido:

> **continuo invadit: "tu nunc Karthaginis altae**
> **fundamenta locas pulchramque uxorius urbem**
> **exstruis? heu!"** (*Aeneid* 4.265)

Vocabulary: *Karthaginis altae*: of lofty Carthage
invadere: to attack, accost
locare: to locate, put, place
exstruere: to construct [in this text, all verbs are present tense]
urbem: city [object]

1. Which word in the text is not necessary and why?

2. What does *-que* mean when attached to a Latin word? Where does it belong in the sentence when you translate it, in relation to the word it is attached to?

3. If the word is *fundamentum -i* (n): "foundation," then *fundamenta* can function as what two things in a Latin sentence and why?

4. Which function is excluded in Vergil's sentence, and why?

5. Find *continuo* and *nunc* in the dictionary, and give a complete translation of Vergil's lines.

6. Using Vergil as inspiration, and some of his vocabulary, say in Latin:

"You immediately attack us and them: you [*pl*] now locate she-goats and wolves here and there [*find "here" and "there" in the dictionary*] and [*expressed in three ways*] you [*pl*] *are* constructing enclosures [*cavea -ae (f)*] and stables [*stabulum -i (n)*] everywhere [*look this up in the dictionary*]."

For style, put the verbs at the end of each phrase and express all pronouns.

D.

hastam <u>alii</u> galeamque ferunt; nam <u>cetera</u> <u>Turnus</u>
<u>victor</u> habet. (*Aeneid* 11.91–92)

Vocabulary: *alius*: another person, man
Turnus: the king of the Latins
victor: victorious
ceterum -i (n): the remaining thing

1. Who exactly is the subject of *ferunt*?

2. Who is the subject of *habet*?

3. What two things does that *-que* join?

4. What does "et cetera" mean?

5. Translate the Latin into English:

6. Write in Latin, expressing all pronouns: "They [women] are carrying them [men] and we have him and her."

LESSON 4

VARIATIONS OF BLOCK 1 NOUNS; BLOCK 1 ADJECTIVES

Variations of Block 1 Nouns

Block 1 nouns normally look like this

ludus -i (m)	*a game*
cura -ae (f)	*a concern, care*
velum -i (n)	*a sail, curtain*

But there are some simple variations:

1. masculine nouns that end in *r* in the subject singular, such as

arbiter, arbitri (m)	*a witness or judge*
vir, viri (m)	*a man*
puer, pueri (m)	*a boy*

- As usual, the second part (the "of-possession" [genitive] singular) still shows you that these nouns belong to the Block 1 family.
- This part also shows you what happens to the word when the ending changes, so put your endings on the stem as shown in the second part. For example, the object singular of *arbiter* is *arbitrum* (not *arbiterum*).

2. masculine nouns that look feminine (about 2 percent of all masculine nouns), such as

agricola -ae (m)	*a farmer*
nauta -ae (m)	*a sailor*
trapezita -ae (m)	*a money changer*

- These nouns share the same endings as Block 1 feminine nouns.
- You must always remember that they are **masculine** when the time comes to describe them with an adjective!

3. feminine nouns that look masculine (about 5 percent of all feminine nouns), such as

   alnus -i (f) *the alder*

- Most of the words for trees in Latin are feminine.

nautas gubernatoresque comparari iubet.

Caesar, *De Bello Gallico* 3.9.1

He orders sailors and pilots to be procured.

- Looking ahead to the next section, how do you think you might describe the *nautas* as "respectable," using the adjective *honestus -a -um*?

Block 1 Adjectives

Fifty percent of all Latin adjectives belong to Block 1. You can identify whether an adjective belongs to this family by how it appears in the dictionary:

saevus -a -um	*savage, cruel*
sanus -a -um	*sound, healthy*
iustus -a -um	*just, righteous*

In each case, the dictionary entry gives you the ending for the masculine, feminine, and neuter singular subject form. The *us a um* pattern tells you that they are Block 1 adjectives, with the same endings as Block 1 nouns (Lesson 2). The masculine adjective can have the same variation as some Block 1 masculine nouns, where the first dictionary entry ends *er*:

asper, aspera, asperum *rough, bitter, desperate*

If you are using an adjective to describe a noun, it will have to agree with it, that is to say, match it, in terms of its function in a sentence (subject, object, "of-possession"), its gender (masculine, feminine, or neuter), and its number (singular or plural). Because of the nature of Latin, however, when you are reading a sentence these adjectives and nouns may be separated by many other words. Train your Latin eye!

bonus dominus	*a good master*
filia bona	*a good daughter*
bonum consilium	*a good plan*
agricola bonus	*a good farmer*
bona populus	*a good poplar tree*
dominus miser	*an unhappy master*
pater bonus est	*the father is good*
magistrum bonum video	*I see a good teacher*
pulchras videmus feminas	*we see beautiful women*

Classical Latin Translation Practice

Publius Vergilius Maro (70–19 AC)

torva leaena lupum sequitur, lupus ipse capellam,
florentem cytisum sequitur lasciva capella,
te Corydon, o Alexi: trahit sua quemque voluptas.
aspice, aratra iugo referunt suspensa iuvenci,
et sol crescentis decedens duplicat umbras;
me tamen urit amor: quis enim modus adsit amori?

Ecloga 2.63–68

Vocabulary:
sequitur: he/she/it pursues or goes after
florentem: flowering (object)
cytisus -i (c): a shrubby kind of clover
Corydon and *Alexis*: [lovers in the poem]
trahit: [present tense]
quemque: each one
voluptas (feminine subject): desire
aspice: look!
iugo: from the yoke
referunt: [present tense]
suspensus -a -um: suspended
sol . . . decedens: setting sun
duplicat: [present tense]
crescentis: growing, lengthening
urit: [present tense]
adsit: may there be?
amori: to love

1. Using lines 1 and 2 of Vergil's Latin, and changing the verb from *sequitur* to *sequntur*, say in Latin: "The fierce lionesses pursue the wolves, the wolves the she-goats, the frisky she-goats the clovers."

2. Using line 4, and changing the verb from *referunt* to *retulit*, say in Latin: "The young bullock has brought back the plough."

3. Using line 5, say in Latin: "They double the shadow."

Publius Ovidius Naso (43 AC–17/18 PC)

Primus sollicitos <u>fecisti</u>, <u>Romule</u>, ludos,
<u>Cum</u> <u>iuvit</u> viduos <u>rapta</u> <u>Sabina</u> viros.
Tunc neque <u>marmoreo</u> pendebant vela <u>theatro</u>,
Nec <u>fuerant</u> <u>liquido</u> pulpita rubra <u>croco</u>.

Ars Amatoria 1.101–4

Vocabulary:
fecisti: [simple past tense verb (*facio*)]
Romule: O Romulus
cum: when
iuvit: [simple past tense verb (*iuvo*)]
rapta: having been snatched
Sabina: Sabine woman
marmoreo … theatro: in the marble theatre
fuerant: had been
liquido … croco: with liquid saffron

1. Using your Latin eyes, find the adjectives that describe *ludos*, *viros*, and *pulpita*.

2. Reverse (singular to plural, or vice versa) each noun-adjective pair.

3. Now reverse the phrase *pendebant vela*.

4. Believe! You can translate the whole thing! (Don't forget to use the vocabulary!)

Post-Classical Latin Translation Practice

Petrus Bembo (1470–1547 PC)

Namque ut habent mala rura valentes saepe colonos,
Pigraque, qui bonus est, otia sentit ager,
Sic non formosae cultu nituerunt puellae,
Et quae pulchra, eadem desidiosa fuit. . . .
Tantum animo, quantum, Borgia, fronte micas.

Carmina 12 *Ad Lucretiam Borgia*

Vocabulary: *ut*: just as
rura: [look up *rus* (remember your neuter super rules!)]
valentes (masculine object plural): strong, capable
qui: which
cultu: with cultivation, adornment
quae: the one who is
eadem: that same one
tantum animo, quantum fronte: as much in soul as in appearance

1. Look up the following verbs in the dictionary: *habeo, sum, sentio, mico*. Now give the meaning of the present tense forms of those verbs in the text: *habent, est, sentit, micas.*

2. Look up the verb *niteo*. Remembering the meaning also of *sum*, give the meaning of the past tense forms of those verbs in the text: *nituerunt, fuit.*

3. What is ambiguous about the function of the words *mala rura*?

4. What is the clear function of the words *valentes … colonos*? How will this help you solve the problem of the first line?

5. What is ambiguous about the function of the words *pigra … otia*?

6. How does looking at the verb in line 2 solve this ambiguity?

7. Which common variation of Block 1 masculine nouns does *ager* exemplify? Look up the noun *ager* in the dictionary and give the reverse form. Which two Latin adjectives in the lines show the same variation?

8. How are the *puellae* described in line 3? Look very carefully at the Latin!

9. Say in Latin, using three different ways of saying "and": "The lazy farmers have sluggish fields, and the good girls shone with cultivation, and we glitter in soul and in appearance."

LESSON 5

ADJECTIVES AS NOUNS

Adjectives standing alone can be translated as nouns. To express the idea "righteous men" in Latin, you do not need the noun for "men" since, in Latin, the ending on the adjective can tell you the gender, number, and function of the person or people with that characteristic. This practice, of using just the single adjective for a noun expression, is very common in Latin and produces a beautiful brevity, but may slow you down in your reading, since only careful analysis will provide the correct English translation. You will need many more words in English to bring out the full meaning of the Latin:

ADJECTIVES ON THEIR OWN ACT AS NOUNS

Masculine singular: add the word "man / person"
Feminine singular: add the word "woman"
Neuter singular: add the word "thing"
Masculine plural: add the word "men / people"
Feminine plural: add the word "women"
Neuter plural: add the word "things"

iusti iusta faciunt	*just men do just things*
iusta iusta facit	*the just woman does just things*
iustae iustos vident	*the just women see just men*
et cetera	*and the other things*

Classical Latin Translation Practice

Quintus Horatius Flaccus (65–8 AC)

invidus, iracundus, <u>iners</u>, vinosus, amator,
nemo adeo ferus est, <u>ut</u> non <u>mitescere</u> <u>possit</u>.

Epistulae 1.1.38

Vocabulary: *iners, inertis* (adjective): indolent, inactive
ut: that
mitescere: to grow mild
possit: he is able

1. What do we know about adjectives standing on their own in a sentence? Therefore, what word can you add to each of the first four words of the first line, to bring out this list of "types"?

<u>expertus</u> <u>metuet</u>. (*Epistulae* 1.18.87)

Vocabulary: *expertus -a -um*: experienced
metuet: [future tense verb]

1. Say in Latin: "The experienced women will fear"; "You, an experienced woman, will fear."

plerumque modestus occupat obscuri speciem, taciturnus acerbi.

Epistulae 1.18.94–95

Vocabulary: *plerumque*: generally
occupare: to take on
speciem (object): appearance

1. What word must you add in translating the adjectives *modestus* and *taciturnus* to bring out the meaning fully?

2. What other function can the *-i* ending for masculine Block 1 nouns indicate, if it is *not* subject plural? Look back at how nouns are presented, in their dictionary forms, in Lesson 2. Use the alternative function to translate *obscuri* and *acerbi*.

inter cuncta leges et percontabere doctos.

Epistulae 1.18.96

Vocabulary: *inter* (preposition + object): among
leges: [future tense verb]
pecontabere: you will question
doctus -a -um: learned

1. If the preposition *inter* is always followed by an object form, then what gender and number must *cuncta* be? What word do you need to add in translation to bring out its meaning fully?

2. What word needs to be added to bring out the full meaning of *doctos*?

3. Say in Latin: "You will question things among all men and women"—use two ways of saying "and."

Post-Classical Latin Translation Practice

Biblia Vulgata, Hieronymus (347–420 PC)

deficere facitis egenos terrae. (Amos 8.4)

Vocabulary: *deficere*: to fail, disappear
facitis: [present tense verb (*facio*—cause)]

1. What other function can the *-ae* ending for feminine Block 1 nouns indicate, if it is *not* subject plural? Look back at how nouns are presented, in their dictionary forms, in Lesson 2. Use this alternative function to translate *terrae*.

2. What do we know about adjectives standing on their own in a sentence? Therefore, what word will you add to your translation of *egenos* to bring out the meaning fully?

aperiemus frumentum, ut imminuamus mensuram,
et augeamus siclum, et supponamus stateras dolosas,
ut possideamus in argento egenos.

Amos 8.5–6

Vocabulary: *aperiemus*: [future tense verb]
ut: so that . . . may
imminuere: to lessen
augere: to increase
siclus -i (m): shekel
supponere: to place underneath
statera -ae (f): balance, scales
possidere: to possess
in argento: in silver

1. Translate the main verb *aperiemus*. What is its object? Say in Latin: "they will open"; "you (sing) will open."

2. Which adjective in this text is used as a noun? Using this adjective, say in Latin: "The destitute woman will open the destitute things." Then say: "They may increase the shekels."

Aurelius Ambrosius (340–397 PC)

Ergo sancti ascendunt ad dominum, flagitiosi ad vitia descendunt, sancti in montibus, criminosi in vallibus, deus enim montium est et non deus vallium.

Epistulae 12 *Ambrosius Irenaeo Salutem* 2

Vocabulary: *ascendunt* and *descendunt*: [present tense verbs]
in montibus / vallibus: in the mountains / valleys
montium / vallium: of mountains / of valleys

1. Fleshing out the full meaning of the adjectives by making them into nouns, who are the *sancti*, *flagitiosi*, and *criminosi*?

LESSON 6

THE SEVEN FUNCTIONS OF NOUNS; PREPOSITIONS FOLLOWED BY THE "OBJECT" FUNCTION

Nouns, adjectives, and pronouns have seven possible functions (and their equivalent endings) in any sentence.

Three functions we have met already:

1. **Subject** (the person doing the verb): the *nominative*
2. **Object** (the person or thing receiving the direct action of an active verb): the *accusative*
3. **Of-Possession**: the *genitive*

Two other common functions:

4. **To-for-from** (the indirect object): the *dative*
5. **By-with-from-in**: the *ablative*

Two less common functions:

6. **Direct address**: the *vocative*
7. **Place where**: the *locative*

Prepositions Followed by the "Object" Function (Accusative)

A preposition describes where things are in relation to each other.

The chicken walked *across* the road.

As well as denoting the person or thing receiving the direct action of an active verb, the object function (*accusative*) is also used after half of all Latin prepositions. The dictionary will always indicate this ("prep. with acc."). The noun in the accusative is said to be the "object" of the preposition.

First, four "special" prepositions. These are always followed by the accusative when a sense of motion (physical or moral) is indicated. These four prepositions are special because, when there is no sense of motion involved (i.e., when they are describing where something is positioned), they are followed by the ablative function (see Lesson 25).

The Four Special Prepositions

in	*into, onto, to, for, against, unto*
sub	*under*
subter	*under*
super	*above*

dum vitant stulti vitia, in contraria currunt.

Quintus Horatius Flaccus, *Sermones* 1.2.24

While stupid people avoid vices, they run into the opposite things/vices.

Other Prepositions Followed by the Object Function (Accusative Case)

ad	*to, up to, towards, at, for, with regard to, according to*
adversus	*toward or against [in either a movement or a moral sense]*
ante	*before [time], in front of [place]*
apud	*among, with, at the house of, before, around, in the works of, according to*
circum, circa, circiter	*around [place or time]*
cis	*on this side of*
citra	*on the near side of, short of*
contra	*against*
erga	*toward [moral relationships* not *of place]*
extra	*outside of*
infra	*below*
inter	*among (many), between (two)*
intra	*within*
iuxta	*next to, according to [ecclesiastical Latin only]*
ob	*in front of, because of*
penes	*in the power of*
per	*through, along, across, with the help of, through the instrumentality of*
post	*after [time], behind [place]*
praeter	*beyond, besides, with the exception of*
prope	*near (also means almost)*
propter	*on account of, because of*
secundum	*according to [later iuxta]*
supra	*above*
trans	*across, over, beyond*
ultra	*beyond*

non est ad astra mollis e terris via

The road from the earth to the stars is not soft

per aspera ad astra

Through difficult things to the stars

As a matter of style, the preposition is never placed after the noun. Where an adjective describes the noun, the preposition is often placed between the adjective and noun:

quam ob rem	*on account of which thing*
tua propter merita	*on account of your services*

Translation Toolkit[1]

It's never too early to start learning the logical steps for translating sentences from Latin into English. Sometimes the meaning might be obvious, sometimes not. If it's not obvious, this is how to avoid mistakes caused by guessing or going too fast.

Remember your rules from Lesson 1:

i. Know your vocabulary as it appears in the dictionary. If you don't know, look it up.
ii. Read the entire sentence; never start with the first word.
iii. Train your Latin eye to analyze the endings.

After that, you need to find the main building blocks of the sentence as it flows in English—namely subject, verb, object—and fill in from there. Start with the verb, because it will make finding the subject easier.

i. Find the **main verb**. For now, work out who is doing it. When possible, work out the verb time. Translate it.
ii. Look for nouns, adjectives, and pronouns with **subject endings**. These words are doing the verb.
iii. If it's a verb that takes an object, look for nouns, adjectives, and pronouns with **object endings**. They will be receiving the direct action of the verb.
iv. Look for prepositions and their objects. These form discrete **prepositional phrases**, although the preposition and its object(s) may not be sitting conveniently next to each other!
v. Fill in the other details—at this stage **adverbs** (look them up in the dictionary) or **of-possession (genitive) endings**.

1. See also Reference Sheet 3.

Classical Latin Translation Practice

Gaius Valerius Catullus (84–54 AC)

Multas per gentes et multa per aequora vectus
advenio has miseras, frater, ad inferias.

Carmina 101.1–2

Vocabulary: *gentes* (noun object): peoples
aequor (neuter noun): sea
vectus -a -um: having traveled
has: these

1. Identify the main verb and its subject. It's in the present tense. Which adjective in the sentence is agreeing with the subject?

2. Identify the three prepositional phrases, each three words long.

3. How would you rewrite the lines replacing *et* with *-que*?

ad solam dominam usque pipiabat.
qui nunc it per iter tenebricosum

Carmina 3.10–11

Vocabulary: *usque*: continually
qui: which [sparrow]
it: [present tense verb from *eo, ire* ...]

1. The main verb is *pipiabat*. This is the continuous past tense of *pipio*. What does it mean?

2. Point out two prepositional phrases in these lines.

Publius Vergilius Maro (70–19 AC)

in flammas et in arma feror.

Aeneid 2.337

Vocabulary: *feror*: I rush

1. Learn now, once and for all, the six meanings for *in* when followed by the object function (and "in" isn't one of them!).

2. Why is the preposition *in* special, and which three other prepositions work in this way?

revocare gradum superasque evadere ad auras
hoc opus, hic labor est.

Aeneid 6.128–29

Vocabulary: *revocare*: to retrace
evadere: to come out, escape
hoc and *hic*: this

Post-Classical Latin Translation Practice

An ancient Latin hymn featured in *Liturgia Romana*, Paulus VI (1897–1978 PC)

Sub tuum praesidium confugimus, sancta Dei Genetrix. . . .

1. Why is the preposition *sub* special? What is important to remember about it when it is followed by the object function? Which three other prepositions work in this way?

2. Identify the main verb here and translate it (present tense).

3. If the word in the dictionary is *deus, dei* (m), then what two possible meanings does *dei* have?

Carolus M. Schulz (1922–2000 PC)

"Osculum in nasum positum magnopere iram avertit!"

Vocabulary: *positus -a -um*: having been placed
avertit: [present tense verb]

1. Learn now, once and for all, six meanings for *in* when followed by the object function (and "in" isn't one of them!).

2. Hunt around in your dictionary and find the meaning of the adverb *magnopere.*

3. Say in Latin: "We holy women on account of [preposition list] your savage [*saevus -a -um*] anger placed [*posuimus*] wet [*umidus -a -um*] kisses onto your great [*magnus -a -um*] noses." (Place prepositions between nouns and adjectives.)

Florens Tertullianus (160–220 PC)

Ad omnem progressum atque promotum, ad omnem aditum et exitum, ad vestitum et calciatum, ad lavacra, ad mensas, ad lumina, ad cubilia, ad sedilia, quaecumque nos conversatio exercet frontem crucis signaculo terimus.

De Corona Militis c.3

Vocabulary: *quaecumque ... conversatio*: whatever habit [subject]
exerceo: I keep busy
tero: I wear away
frontem (noun object): forehead
signaculo: with the sign

1. Which function-case follows the preposition *ad*? Hopefully, you will identify a long list of nouns in this function here. Which are singular (sing) and which are plural (pl)?

2. Focus on the verb in the phrase beginning *quaecumque*, and identify the function of the word *nos*. Give the reverse form.

3. From the unusual-looking noun (we will learn about these sorts of nouns in Lesson 13) *crux, crucis* (m), what is the meaning of *crucis*, according to how nouns are presented in the dictionary in Latin?

LUDUS 2

AFTER LESSONS 4–6

Topics covered: *variations of Block 1 nouns; Block 1 adjectives; adjectives as nouns; the seven functions; prepositions with the accusative.*

The greatest scholar and encyclopedist of the seventh century PC was the Archbishop of Seville, Spain, Isidorus Hispalensis (560–636 PC), who collected all the knowledge of the world at that time into his twelve books on *Etymologies*, where he has some funny things, some incredible, from soup to nuts, from God to apes.

A.

Nostri prophetas vocant, quasi praefatores quia ... vera praedicunt ... / ... in veteri testamento ... videbant ea quae ceteri non videbant, et praespiciebant quae in mysterio abscondita erant.

7.8.1

Vocabulary: *propheta -ae* (m): prophet
praefatores: people who speak in advance
in veteri testamento and *in mysterio*: in the old testament, in a mystery
quae (n pl): which
ceterus -a -um: rest, other, remaining
absconditus -a -um: hidden

1. If the word *nostri* is a form of *noster, nostra, nostrum* (our, ours), then to which block does it belong?

2. What is special or irregular about it?

3. What word do you have to add to the form *nostri* on its own in the text, to bring out the full meaning?

4. What does *ceteri* mean on its own?

5. The verbs in the text are *vocare*: to call; *praedicere*: to predict (present tense in text); *videre*: to see; *praespicere*: to foresee; *esse*: to be (past tense in text). Translate Isidorus's sentence.

6. What do the following expressions mean:

   a. *nos prophetae vocant*

   b. *nostros prophetas vocant*

   c. *nostras prophetae vocant*

   d. *nostrae prophetas vocant*

On November 10, the universal church celebrates the yearly feast day of one of the really great shepherds of old, Leo Magnus, bishop of Rome, 440–461 PC, who has left us not only basic dogmas about the nature of Christ but also the most melodious, polished, elegant Latinity of all the Latin church fathers. Here is some for your education and imitation.

B.

On the day of his election as supreme pontiff, September 29, 440, he said the following:

non verecundae sed ingratae mentis indicium est beneficia tacere divina.

Sermo 1.1

Vocabulary: *verecundae . . . ingratae mentis*: of a modest . . . of an ungrateful mind
est: it is
tacere: to be silent about

1. Find in the dictionary and tell the difference between *iudicium* and *indicium*.

2. Translate the line.

3. Reverse (singular to plural or vice versa): *indicium* and *divina*.

C.

One of Leo's famous Christological formulae, written on the third anniversary of his election, September 29, 443:

> **divinitatem usque ad humana submisit, humanitatem usque ad divina provexit.**
>
> Sermo 3.2

Vocabulary: *divinitatem … humanitatem*: divine nature … human nature (objects)
submittere: to subject, submit
provehere: advance, promote [verbs past tense here]

1. Give several meanings for the Latin preposition *ad*.

2. If the adjectives are *humanus -a -um* (human) and *divinus -a -um* (divine), then what gender and number do you see in the text (following *ad* …)?

3. Therefore, what word do we have to add in English to bring out the full meaning?

4. Translate the line.

5. Follow Leo's word order and write in Latin: "Through [see preposition list] Latin studies [*studium -i* (n)] we humans have not subjected divine persons to our human things, but we have advanced human persons to divine regions [*provincia -ae* (f)]."

D.

et tamen non desperamus neque deficimus . . . et davidicum psalmum—dilectissimi—non ad nostrum elationem sed ad Christi Domini gloriam consona voce cantavimus.

Sermo 3.1

Vocabulary: *desperare*: to despair
deficere: to fail [both *desperare* and *deficere* are present tense here]
davidicus -a -um: davidical, of King David, the supposed author of the psalms in the bible
dilectissimi: O most beloved!
elationem: exaltation [object here]
consona voce: with harmonious voice
cantare: to sing [past tense here]

1. What is the function of *davidicum psalmum* in the sentence above? Explain fully.

2. What function-case follows the preposition *ad*?

3. Which words in the text are objects of the preposition *ad*?

4. If the dictionary entries read *Christus -i* (m): Christ, and *Dominus -i* (m): Lord, then which possible functions do you see in the words *Christi Domini*?

5. Which will you choose for your translation and why?

6. Translate the Latin.

7. Use all your learning so far to write in Latin: "You [pl] are not despairing because of [use two different prepositions] a rough [*asper, aspera, asperum*] teacher [*magistra, magistrae* (f)] nor are you failing because of first [*primus -a -um*] impediments [*impedimentum -i* (n)] but you have sung [pl T.4 **special] davidical psalms next to your [*vester, vestra, vestrum*] colleagues [*collega -ae* (m)]."

For best Latin style, put prepositional phrases out in front of their clauses, with the preposition between the noun and the adjective.

LESSON 7

THE SIX TIMES IN THE INDICATIVE

Time	*One Latin Example*	*English Meanings*
Time 1 *present tense*	**amant**	they love they are loving they do love
Time 2 *imperfect tense* continuous, repeated or frustrated action in the past; a moving film	**cantabat**	she was singing she used to sing she would sing she kept singing she tried to sing
Time 3 *future tense*	**venies**	you will come you will be coming
Time 4: one form, two distinct times		
Time 4a *present perfect tense*, a present tense to Romans	**dixi**	I have spoken I have been speaking
Time 4b *past simple/perfect tense* completed action; photo	**dixi**	I spoke I did speak
Time 5 *pluperfect tense*	**videramus**	we had seen we had been seeing
Time 6 *future perfect tense*	**scripseritis**	you will have written you will have been writing

Notes on Times / Tenses

The indicative is the verb mood used to indicate or point things out. It is used for direct statements and questions. The other moods are the imperative and the subjunctive. Whatever time you are reading, the person doing the verb is always recognized in the ending on the verb: **o-m-i / s-sti**/ t / mus / tis-stis** / nt -erunt**** (see Lesson 1). All narration progresses in Time 4b (the simple past) and the whole language revolves around it.

Notice how there are many different options for translating each time. Because of the way some verbs are formed in Latin, and the fact that Time 4 covers two distinct verb times, there are often multiple different possible meanings for one verb form. From the verb *attendo, attendere, attendi, attentus -a -um*, the form *attendit* could have seven possible translations:

TIME 1: ***ATTENDIT***

he/she/it attends
he/she/it is attending
he/she/it does attend

TIME 4A: ***ATTENDIT***

he/she/it has attended
he/she/it has been attending

TIME 4B: ***ATTENDIT***

he/she/it attended
he/she/it did attend

Try not to assume and thus limit the possibilities of your accurate translations: hold the multiple possibilities in your head until you have more evidence to make a single selection.

Classical Latin Reading Practice

Lucius Annaeus Seneca (c. 4–65 PC)

Isti qui per officia *discursant*, qui se aliosque *inquietant*, cum bene *insanierint*, cum omnium limina cotidie *perambulaverint* nec ullas apertas fores *praeterierint*, cum per diversissimas domos meritoriam salutationem *circumtulerint*, quotum quemque ex tam inmensa et variis cupiditatibus districta urbe *poterunt* videre?

De Brevitate Vitae 14

Vocabulary:
iste, ista, istud (think Block 1): this, that
qui: who
se: themselves
cum: when
bene: thoroughly
omnium limina: the thresholds of all people
fores (f pl object): doors
diversissimas domos: various, far-flung homes
salutationem (f sing object): greeting
quotum quemque (object) how few
ex tam immensa et variis cupiditatibus districta urbe: from a city so immense and busy with various desires

1. Give all possible translations of the underlined verbs in the text. The infinitive and time of the verbs is given below.

Infinitive	*Basic verb meaning*	*Time of verb form in text*	*Possible Translations of verb form in text*
discursare	to run about	T.1	
inquietare	to disturb	T.1	
insanire	to act like a madman	T.6	
perambulare	to ramble around	T.6	
praeterire	to go past	T.6	
circumferre	to spread around	T.6	
posse	to be able	T.3	

2. Of the many meanings of *per*, which works in the passage above? It is always followed by which function-case?

3. Say in Latin: "When you [pl] will have rambled around very far-flung houses, we disturb you through our duty."

Post-Classical Latin Reading Practice

Aurelius Augustinus (354–430 PC)

Sero te *amavi*, pulchritudo tam antiqua et tam nova, sero te amavi! et ecce intus *eras* et ego foris, et ibi te *quaerebam*, et in ista formosa, quae *fecisti*, deformis *inruebam*. mecum eras, et tecum non *eram*. ea me *tenebant* longe a te, quae si in te non essent, non essent. *vocasti* et *clamasti* et *rupisti* surditatem meam: *coruscasti*, *splenduisti* et *fugasti* caecitatem meam: fragrasti, et *duxi* spiritum, et *anhelo* tibi, *gustavi* et *esurio* et *sitio*, *tetigisti* me, et *exarsi* in pacem tuam.

Confessiones 10.27

Vocabulary:
mecum: with me
tecum: with you
longe a te: far from you
quae: which (things)
non essent: they did not exist

1. Give all possible translations of the italicized verbs in the text. The infinitive and time of the verbs are given below.

Infinitive	*Basic verb meaning*	*Time of verb form in text*	*Possible Translations of verb form in text*
amare	to love	T.4	
esse	to exist	T.2	
quaerere	to seek	T.2	
facere	to make	T.4	
inruere	to rush	T.2	
tenere	to hold	T.2	
vocare	to call	T.4	
clamare	to shout	T.4	
rumpere	to force open	T.4	
coruscare	to glitter	T.4	
splendere	to shine	T.4	
fugare	to chase away	T.4	
fragrare	to emit a fragrance	T.4	
ducere	to draw	T.4	
anhelare	to pant	T.1	

Infinitive	*Basic verb meaning*	*Time of verb form in text*	*Possible Translations of verb form in text*
gustare	to taste	T.4	
esurire	to hunger	T.1	
sitire	to thirst	T.1	
tangere	to touch	T.4	
exardere	to burn	T.4	

2. Give six possible meanings of *in* when followed by the object function-case.

LESSON 8

THE PRINCIPAL PARTS OF VERBS; THE EASY WAY TO FORM TIMES 4-5-6

Latin Verbs in the Dictionary

Group 1 (40%)	[pretty regular]	**paro, parare, paravi, paratus -a -um**	prepare
Group 2 (10%)	[quite irregular]	**habeo, habere, habui, habitus -a -um**	have
		maneo, manere, mansi, mansus -a -um	remain
Group 3 (40%)	[totally irregular]	**dico, dicere, dixi, dictus -a -um**	say
Group 4 (10%)	[pretty regular]	**audio, audire, audivi, auditus -a -um**	hear

All Latin verbs have principal parts (PPs), usually four, which enable you to do everything with the verb that the verb can do. The four principal parts will be written out in full in the dictionary, or the dictionary will indicate that the verb follows a regular pattern, which you will get to know. For example, most Group 1 verbs follow the regular pattern *-o*, *-are*, *-avi*, *-atus*, so the dictionary will not necessarily write this all out, instead just denoting the group number in brackets: *paro* (1). Sometimes a verb does not have a third or fourth part. This will also be clear from the dictionary.

The principal parts have fixed meanings, outlined in the following table:

The Meaning of the Principal Parts

PP1—I (*ego*) *present tense* TIME 1	PP2—"to . . ." *the infinitive*	PP3—I (*ego*) *perfect tense* TIME 4	PP4—"having been -ed" *passive past participle*
audio I hear I am hearing I do hear	*audire** to hear	*audivi* I have heard I have been hearing I heard I did hear	*auditus -a -um*† having been heard Notice how this PP has Block 1 endings and is an *adjective*.

*PP2 may also be translated "hearing." The infinitive is one way of expressing the **gerund** in Latin, a neuter noun in the subject and object function. It does not change its ending.

†PP4 is called, officially, the **supine**. Gerunds and supines come much later. . . .

The Easy Way to Form Times 4-5-6

Whatever time you are reading, the person doing the verb is always recognized in the ending on the verb: **o-m-i / s-sti**/ t / mus / tis -stis** / nt -erunt****. In order to form the perfect tenses, Times 4-5-6, take the stem from the third principal part (PP3) in the dictionary and add the appropriate endings, shown in the table below. Take, for instance, the verb *audire*, "to hear."

audio, audire, *audivi*, auditus

The PP3 stem is *audivi* (you will drop the final *-i* in certain circumstances).

T.4 PP3 + ** T.4 specials	PP3 **Add T.4 special person endings** (NB: drop the *-i* for "they")	audivi audivisti** audivit	audivimus audivistis** audiv**erunt****
T.5 **PP3 + -era-** **(think: had)**	PP3 **Take away the *-i*** **Add *-era-* and person endings**	audiveram audiveras audiverat	audiveramus audiveratis audiverant
T.6 **PP3 + -eri-** **(think: will have)**	PP3 **Take away the *i*** **Add *-eri-* and person endings** (NB 'I' = *-ero* not *-eri*)	audiv**ero** audiveris audiverit	audiverimus audiveritis audiverint

** T.4 "they" *-erunt* is often shortened to *-ere*: *audiverunt* becomes *audivere*. You know this is not PP2 because of the PP3 stem.

Notes

- All verbs in the language form Times 4-5-6 in this way. There are no exceptions.
- Because there is one pattern for all verbs, you do not need to write out tables for different verbs.
- It can be time consuming to realize that you are looking at a PP3 stem, and work out which verb it is. In the early days, you have to hunt in the dictionary, and learn your vocabulary! This is a

lifetime's work, but the best possible way to become independent and fluent in the language. Try and find: *cecini*; *sustuli*; *pepuli* (hint: look under *can*; *tol*; *pel*).

Cornelius Tacitus (56–120 PC)

huic mulieri cuncta alia *fuere* praeter honestum animum.

Annales 13.45.7

To this woman there were all other things except an honorable character.

Classical Latin Translation Practice

Gaius Julius Caesar (100–44 AC)

veni, vidi, vici!

1. Give all possible translations of this famous phrase.

2. Write in Latin (and see how one little letter makes all the difference): "They had come, they saw, they will have conquered!"

3. What is the fancy, contracted version of "they saw"?

Two Extant Letters from Caesar to Cicero

praeterire tamen non potui. (*Ad Atticum* 9.6a.1)

Vocabulary: *praeterire*: [from *praetereo*]

1. Say in Latin: "You [pl] were not able to go past"; "You [sing] had been able to hear us however"; "I will have been able to conquer."

hoc et feci saepe. (*Ad Atticum* 9.6a.1)

Vocabulary: *hoc*: this (neuter)

1. What can *et* mean when it doesn't mean "and"? (Look back at Lesson 3)

2. What is the difference between *fecere* and *facere*? What is the difference between *fecerant* and *fecerunt*? One letter in Latin makes all the difference in the world.

amicitiae graviorem iniuriam feceris et tibi minus commode consulueris.

Ad Atticum 10.8b.1

Vocabulary: *amicitiae*: to our friendship
graviorem (object): rather serious
tibi: your own interests (after *consulo*)
minus: less

1. Look in the dictionary under the adjective *commodus -a -um* and take note of a few of its meanings. There you should find also the meaning of the adverb *commode*.

2. Say in Latin: "We will not have been able to pass by although [*quamquam*] he had often done convenient things [one word!], and you [pl] wrote such [*tam*] long letters."

Post-Classical Latin Translation Practice

Heloisa Diaconissa (1101–1164 PC)

Missam ad amicum . . . epistolam, dilectissime, vestram ad me forte quidam nuper attulit.

Heart-breaking "Letter 2" from Heloise to Abelard

Vocabulary: *dilectissime*: most beloved
quidam (subject) a certain person

1. From the verb *mitto, mittere, misi, missus* (send), what does PP4 *missam* mean, and what noun is it describing in the Latin above? Which other word in the line describes this noun?

2. What function-case follows the preposition *ad*? Which noun is the object of the first *ad*? And the second?

3. Where in the dictionary do you find the word *attulit*? You may have to search for a very long time! (Hint: look under *aff.*)

4. Reverse the whole line (*quidam* stays the same) and then translate your new Latin.

Ardentius eam coepi legere.

Vocabulary: *ardentius*: more ardently

---

1. From the verb *lego, legere, legi, lectus* (read), what does PP2 *legere* mean?

---

2. If *eam* is feminine, why can it legitimately be translated as *it* here?

Nihil umquam, Deus scit, in te nisi te requisivi, te . . . non tua concupiscens.

Vocabulary: *scire*: to know (T.1)
in te: in you
concupiscens (adjective, subject): longing for

---

1. Derived from the adjective *tuus -a -um*, what does the word *tua* mean on its own in this sentence?

---

2. Give the T.5 and T.6 forms of *requisivi*, keeping the subject the same.

Non matrimonii foedera, non dotes aliquas exspectavi, non denique meas voluptates aut voluntates sed tuas, sicut ipse nosti adimplere studui.

Vocabulary: *foedera* (object): contracts
dotes aliquas (object) any dowries
voluptates (f object pl): wishes

1. From the noun *matrimonium, matrimonii* (n): marriage, what is the only possible function and therefore meaning of *matrimonii*? (Look at Lesson 2 if you get stuck.)

2. Write out the principal parts of the verb *[ad]impleo* (= I fulfill), and give the meaning of each principal part.

3. Of which verb are *meas voluptates aut voluntates* the object?

4. Given the ending *-sti*, what are the time and subject of *nosti* (from the verb *noscere*: to get to know)? Give the reverse form.

5. Keeping the subject the same, give the T.1, T.5, and T.6 forms of *studui* and all possible translations.

LESSON 9

THE VERB "TO BE"

The verb "to be" is one of the most commonly used verbs in Latin, and is irregular in all languages. The Latin principal parts of "to be" are *sum, esse, fui.* These have the same fixed meanings as all other principal parts.

Just as in all other verbs, in *esse*, Times 4, 5, and 6 may be formed and recognized at a glance from the third principal part. Times 1-2-3 are slightly less obvious, but still involve forms with which you are already familiar. Whatever time you are reading, the person doing the verb is always recognized in the ending on the verb: **o-m-i / s-sti**/ t / mus / tis-stis** / nt-erunt**.**

Here is a bonus participle: *futurus -a -um* means "about to be," "going to be."

Time 1 *present tense*	**sum es est** **sumus estis sunt**	I am, you are, he/she/it is we are, you [pl] are, they are
Time 2 *imperfect tense*	**eram eras erat** **eramus eratis erant**	I was, you were ...
Time 3 *future tense*	**ero eris erit** **erimus eritis erunt**	I will be, you will be ...

SOME NOTES ABOUT "TO BE"

- With the verb "to be," and similar verbs such as "to stay" and "to become" or "to appear," there is no direct object.
- In the sentences "I am happy" or "I feel happy," both "I" and "happy" are the subject form (nominative case).
- With the verb "to be" in the third person, you can often use the translation "there" for the subject as well as "he/she/it/they": *est*: "there is"; *sunt*: "there are."

olim erat puella. puella erat misera. erunt tamen liberi qui linguam Latinam amant.

Once upon a time, there was a girl. The girl was wretched. However, there will be children who love Latin!

The Verb "To Be *Able*"

The principal parts of this verb, and the formation of Times 4-5-6, operate just like all other verbs: *possum, posse, potui,* to be able, to have power, can.

The first principal part derives from *potis sum*, "I am capable." You will see how what you know about the verb *sum, esse, fui* and your knowledge of person endings, is sufficient to help you recognize Times 1-2-3 of *possum, posse, potui.*

Use that knowledge to fill in the gaps in the chart below:

Time 1	**possum** *I am able*	**possumus** *we are able*
	potes *you are able*	**potestis** *you (pl) are able*
	potest *he/she/it is able*	**possunt** *they are able*
Time 2	**poteram** *I was able*	________ *we were able*
	poteras *you were able*	________ *you (pl) were able*
	________ *he/she/ it was able*	________ *they were able*
Time 3	**potero** *I will be able*	________ *we will be able*
	poteris *you will be able*	________ *you (pl) will be able*
	________ *he/she/it will be able*	**poterunt** *they will be able*

Renatus Cartesius (1596–1650 PC)

ego cogito, ergo sum.

Principia Philosophiae I 1644 (7)

I think, therefore I am.

• Write in Latin:

1. "We thought, therefore we were"

____

____

2. "You [pl] had thought, therefore you [pl] are"

3. "They will have thought, therefore they will be"

possumus dubitare

We are able to doubt

1. Say in Latin (using different ways of saying "and"): "You [sing] are able and you [pl] were able and they will be able to doubt."

2. Reminding yourself of what you learned in Lesson 8, can you generate the principal parts of *dubito* (1)—without looking them up?

3. Now say in Latin: "Although [*quamquam*] other people [*alius -a -um* (one word!)] had doubted, we did not doubt."

Classical Latin Translation Practice

Translate these short phrases from Marcus Tullius Cicero (106–43 AC), *Epistulae ad Atticum*. Then write the modified phrases in your own Latin.

Lepta noster mirificus est. (5.17.2)

Vocabulary: *Lepta*: the name of a Roman

1. "Our things are extraordinary"

reliqua sunt domestica. (5.21.14)

Vocabulary: *domesticus -a -um*: belonging to the household, domestic

1. "The other people were not able to be domestic"

mihi nihil potest esse gratius. (9.9.1)

Vocabulary: *mihi*: to me
gratius: more welcome

1. "Nothing will be able to be more welcome"

scies quicquid erit. (10.12.4)

Vocabulary: *scies*: [T.3]
quicquid (object): whatever

1. "You [pl] will know whatever we will be"

non possum plura scribere. (11.2.3)

Vocabulary: *plus* (neuter): more

1. "They will not be able to know more things"

nec audent nec iam possunt. (15.10)

Vocabulary: *audent*: [T.1 (*audeo*)]

1. "You [sing] are not able to dare, nor will they be able"

Gaius Valerius Catullus (84–54 AC)

Disertissime Romuli nepotum,
quot sunt quotque fuere, Marce Tulli,
quotque post aliis erunt in annis,
gratias tibi maximas Catullus
agit pessimus omnium poeta.

Carmina 49

Vocabulary: *disertissime*: most eloquent
nepotum: of the descendants
quot: however many
Marce Tulli: O Cicero!
aliis … in annis: in other years
gratias … agere: to render thanks [T.1]
tibi: to you
maximus -a -um: greatest
pessimus -a -um: worst
omnium: of all

1. If there was only one founder of Rome, what must *Romuli* mean?

2. The form *fuere* is a contracted form of what verb time? (Lesson 8)

3. Catullus describes himself as *pessimus poeta*. How is it possible that those two words agree, despite their very different endings? (Lesson 4)

Post-Classical Latin Translation Practice

Translate these short phrases from the Biblia Vulgata Liber Psalmorum. Then write the modified phrases in your own Latin.

magna est usque ad caelos misericordia tua. (108.5)

1. "The teacher showed [*praebeo* ...] great pity towards [see the list of prepositions in Lesson 6] the students [*discipulus -i* (m)]."

super me sunt, Deus, vota tua. (56.13)

1. "Our wish will be over the altar [*ara*, *arae* (f)]"

<u>confringebam</u> <u>illos</u>, nec poterant stare. (18.39)

Vocabulary: *confringebam*: [T.2]
ille, *illa*, *illud*: that

1. "I will have smashed those things, nor will they be able to stand"

quoniam circumdederunt me mala, quorum non est numerus; comprehenderunt me iniquitates meae, et non potui videre. (40.13)

Vocabulary: *quorum*: of which
iniquitates (feminine subject): sins, unreasonableness

1. "Because my faults had surrounded me, they were not able to help me"

laudabo Dominum in vita mea, psallam Deo meo, quamdiu fuero. (146.2)

Vocabulary: *laudabo*: [T.3]
psallare: to sing a psalm [T.3]
Deo meo: to my God
quamdiu: as long as

1. "As long as we will have existed, we will be able to praise leisure [*otium -i* (n)]."

Aurelius Augustinus (354–430 PC)

Eris opus Dei, non solum quia homo es, sed etiam quia iustus es. Melius est enim iustum esse, quam te hominem esse. Si hominem te fecit Deus, et iustum tu te facis; melius aliquid facis quam fecit Deus. Sed sine te fecit te Deus. Non enim adhibuisti aliquem consensum, ut te faceret Deus. Quomodo consentiebas qui non eras? Qui ergo fecit te sine te, non te iustificat sine te. Ergo fecit nescientem, iustificat volentem.

Sermo 169.11

Vocabulary:
quia: because
melius … quam: better … than
homo (subject) and *hominem* (object): a human
facis: [T.1 (*facere*)]
aliquid: something
sine te: without you
aliquem: some, any
ut: so that
faceret: he/she/it might make
qui: who
[te] *nescientem* (object): you not knowing
[te] *volentem* (object): you willing

1. From the verb *adhibere* (to use, employ), give the four possible translations of *adhibuisti*, labeling them with their specific time frames as set out in Lesson 7. Do the same for *fecit* (*facere*) and reverse (sing to pl, or vice versa) each Latin verb.

2. Translate the phrase *iustum tu te facis*. Reverse the whole phrase. How would the phrases change if the "you" was specifically female?

3. If *consentiebas* (*consentire*: to agree) is T.2, give at least five possible translations for that verb. What is the difference between T.2 and T.4?

4. Say in Latin using only six Latin words: "You, just woman, are doing just things, and you just men are justifying yourselves."

LUDUS 3

AFTER LESSONS 7–9

Topics covered: *meaning of the six times; PPs; T.4-5-6; sum & possum.*

One of Rome's two great comic playwrights, Publius Terentius Afer (185–159 AC), gives us some idea and feeling of the Latin street talk of Rome in about 160 AC in some short bits of conversation which you should understand and imitate immediately.

A.

Two old men, Menedemus and Chremes, discuss a rediscovered son and his marriage.

{Me.} nunc me fortunatissimum factum puto esse cum te, gnate, intellego resipisse.
{Ch.} ut errat!
{Me.} te ipsum quaerebam, Chreme: serva . . . filium, me ac familiam . . . invenisti hodie filiam. . . .
{Ch.} nimium illi, Menedeme, indulges. . . .
{Me.} sane volo; nam te scientem faciam quidquid egero.

Heauton 842

Vocabulary: *fortunatissimus -a -um*: extremely fortunate
cum: when
gnate: O son!
resipisse: to have wised up
ut: how much!
ipsum: yourself
serva: keep! save!
illi: to him [i.e., to Clinia, his son]
sane: of course, certainly
scientem: well informed (object)
quidquid: whatever

1. Give several precise meanings of the verb times in the text (unknown times indicated):

   a. *puto* (*putare*: to think)

   b. *intellego* (*intellegere*: to understand)

   c. *errat* (*errare*: to err, make a mistake, T.1)

   d. *quaerebam* (*quaerere*: to seek, T.2)

   e. *invenisti* (*invenire*: to find)

   f. *indulges* (*indulgere*: to be indulgent, T.1)

   g. *volo* (*velle*: to wish, want)

   h. *faciam* (*facere*: to make, T.3)

   i. *egero* (*agere*: to do)

2. From the verb *facio, facere, feci, factus -a -um*, what docs *factum* mean? Which word is it describing here?

3. Now translate the Latin conversation between one very strict and one more lenient father.

4. Reverse the numbers (sing to pl, or vice versa) that you find in the following phrases:

   a. *me fortunatissimum factum puto* [NB—he thinks: *putat*]

   b. *invenisti hodie filiam*

   c. *te ipsum quaerebam*

   d. *indulges*

5. Now write in Latin, using the living Latin from c. 160 AC: "How much are lazy people [*piger, pigra, pigrum*] erring through [use preposition] their [*suus -a -um*] lives [*vita -ae* (f)], when they are indulgent and are not understanding [vowel here will be "u"] the great riches [*divitia -ae* (f)] within [use preposition] Latin letters [*littera -ae* (f)] and Roman monuments [*monumentum -i* (n)]."

B.

On hearing that his wife is ill, Pamphilus (a dodgy husband) has a panicky conversation with his slave, Parmeno. This play is called *The Mother-in-Law*.

{Pam.} interii; cur mihi id non dixti?
{Par.} quia non poteram una omnia.
{Pam.} quid morbi est? {Par.} nescio.
{Pam.} quid? nemon medicum adduxit? {Par.} nescio.

Hecyra 322

Vocabulary:
intereo: I am ruined
mihi: to me
dixti = *dixisti*
quia: because
una omnia: all things at the same time
quid (1): what sort?
quid (2): what?
nemon = *nemo*
adducere: bring, summon

1. Give several precise translations for the verbs in the text (this may involve some hunting around in the dictionary.... Fact of Latin life!):

   a. *interii*

   b. *dixisti*

   c. *poteram*

   d. *est*

   e. *nescio*

   f. *adduxit*

2. From the word *morbus, morbi* (m): illness, what function-case must *morbi* in the text be?

3. Translate the conversation.

C.

Young David confronts Goliath in the historical books of the Biblia Vulgata, Hieronymus (347–420 PC).

> **surrexit itaque David mane et commendavit gregem custodi et onustus abiit, sicut praeceperat Isaias . . . festinavit David et cucurrit ad pugnam adversum Philisteum. et misit manum suam in peram tulitque unum lapidem et funda iecit et percussit Philsteum . . . et cecidit in faciem suam super terram, praevaluitque David adversum Philisteum . . . et interfecit eum praeciditque caput eius.**

1 Reg [1 Sam] 17:20–51

Vocabulary:
mane: in the morning
gregem: flock (object)
custodi: to a guard
onustus -a -um: burdened, weighed down
sicut: just as
pera -ae (f): pouch, bag
lapidem: stone (object)
funda: with a sling-shot
faciem: face (object)
caput eius: his head

1. As a matter of Latin theory, why are you more likely to find more verbs in T.4 than T.2?

2. What is the big problem and difficulty with T.4-5-6, when we recognize them? To save some time, here are the dictionary entries for the verbs in the text: *surgo, commendo, abeo, praecipio, festino, curro, mitto, fero* (!), *iacio, percutio, interficio*, and *praecido*. Sometime, sooner or later, you will have to know all these things as Latinists!

3. Identify the one T.5 verb in the text and translate it.

4. Give an alternative preposition for *adversum Philisteum*.

5. Why is the translation "on / in his face" not enough for *in faciem suam*?

6. Why is the translation "in the bag" not enough for *in peram*?

7. Now translate the bible story.

8. Taking the verbs in the text in order, write in Latin:

a. you [pl] had entrusted

---

b. they went away

---

c. we will have instructed

---

d. I hurried

---

e. you [sing] will have run

---

f. they will have sent

---

g. she had taken

---

h. we threw

---

i. you fell

LESSON 10

THE RELATIVE PRONOUN (SUBJECT AND OBJECT FUNCTION)

The relative pronoun (in Latin, *qui*, *quae*, *quod*, in English, "who, whom, whose, which") *relates* to something outside of its own phrase (the relative clause or box). This something is called the "antecedent."

The man **whom** I met last year emigrated to Australia.
The dog liked the woman **who** was sitting on the bench.
Children **whose** parents read a lot do well at school.

The relative pronoun stands for the antecedent, and therefore will be the **same gender and number as the antecedent.** The antecedent may be a person: I, you, he, etc.

The form of the relative pronoun depends on its function-case **within its own relative clause or box**. This function of the relative pronoun, therefore, may well **not be the same** as the function of the antecedent.

	Antecedent is . . .		
In its own box, relative pronoun is	*Masculine singular*	*Feminine singular*	*Neuter singular*
Subject	**qui**	**quae**	**quod**
Object	**quem**	**quam**	**quod**

	Antecedent is . . .		
In its own box, relative pronoun is	*Masculine plural*	*Feminine plural*	*Neuter plural*
Subject	**qui**	**quae**	**quae**
Object	**quos**	**quas**	**quae**

Notice that the Latin form *quae* could be four different things. Take this opportunity to learn the possibilities: the woman who, the women who, the things which....

Reading Examples

In the following translated reading examples, use the dictionary to analyze the relative pronoun.

- What gender and number is the relative pronoun?
- What is the antecedent?
- What function does the relative pronoun have in its own clause?
- When is *which* or *who* used in the translation?

Lucius Annaeus Seneca Iunior (c. 4 AC–65 PC)

Epistulae Morales ad Lucilium

opiniones quae nos circumsonant repellantur. (94.55)

The opinions which din around us should be rejected.

Omnia quae dicunt, quae turba audiente iactant, aliena sunt. (108.38)

All the things which they say, which they toss about while the crowd listens, are other men's.

Mors, quam pertimescimus ac recusamus, intermittit vitam, non eripit. (36.10)

Death, which we greatly fear and deny, interrupts life, does not take it away.

Biblia Vulgata, Hieronymus (347–420 PC)

Evangelium secundum Iohannem

erat lux vera, quae illuminat omnem hominem. (1.9)

It was the true light, which enlightens each human being.

ego sum panis vivus, qui de caelo descendi. (6.51)

I am the living bread, who came down from heaven.

panis quem ego dabo, caro mea est pro mundi vita. (6.52)

The bread which I shall give, is my flesh for the life of the world.

LESSON 11

MORE ON THE RELATIVE PRONOUN

The Romans loved the relative pronoun, the sound of it, the economy of it, the elegance of it. Relative pronouns are everywhere in Latin. These four principles will help navigate translating relative pronouns. They are at the heart of Latin.

Four Principles

One—Relative Box: The Matryoshka Principle

The first verb that follows the relative pronoun **must go with it**. This forms an unbreakable linguistic capsule or box. Sometimes one box can lurk inside another. The verb that remains outside of the relative box must be the main verb.

This principle of linguistic boxes is central to Latin and is vital to remember when entering the world of complex sentences. The first verb that follows a conjunction introducing a subordinate clause **must go with that conjunction.** Mark your boxes, and start translating with the main verb.

[qui librum {quem heri legimus} scripsisti] auctor es.

You are the author who wrote the book which we read yesterday.

Occasionally a word that belongs "in the box" may be displaced and appear in front of the relative pronoun. Just slip it back in. Sometimes it can be challenging to see where a box closes. Reading practice and familiarity with Latin will help. The basic rule, that *the verb that follows a relative pronoun must go with it,* is a very important one to apply.

Two—Position

The relative box is often positioned out in front of the main sentence. This means that the antecedent, or thing it is relating *back* to, comes after it! When reading Latin, always read the whole sentence before you start translating!

quas heri ad me miserunt ostendo gemmas.

I am showing the jewels which they sent to me yesterday.

quod dixisti, id approbavi.

I approved that which you said.

quem vidi miles in urbe est.

The soldier whom I saw is in the city.

Three—Omission of the Pronoun Antecedent

The Romans loved to omit the antecedent of the relative pronoun if that antecedent was just a pronoun. Take the second example above. The sentence means exactly the same with the pronoun, *id*, omitted, and produces a beautiful economy.

quod dixisti approbavi.

I approved that which you said.

In Latin, you can *infer* what the object of *approbavi* is from the gender and number of *quod*. However, in English, this pronoun will have to be expressed for the translation to be correct, so you have to reconstruct the missing "id" and translate it as "that."

quae cecinit Delia laudamus [______________].

We praise <u>the things</u> which Delia sang.

(supply *ea* as the neuter plural antecedent of *quae*)

quos miles ceperat [______________] solvit rex.

The king released <u>the people</u> whom the soldier had captured.

(supply *eos* as the masculine plural antecedent of *quos*)

Sometimes there is ambiguity:

quae vides video.

I see the things which you see. [*omitted ea*]

I see you, who see. [*omitted te*]

Four—Brevity

Look how many English words we need to bring out the meaning of these five Latin words fully:

qui quos amamus misistis estis.

You are the people who sent the people whom we love.

Classical Latin Translation Practice

Lucius Annaeus Seneca Iunior (c. 4 AC–65 PC)

These one-liners are taken from Seneca's blood-drenched tragedy *Thyestes*. In each case, identify the relative pronoun and the verb that goes with it. Think about the relative "box" or clause. Then find the main verb and start translating the main clause first.

quos cogit metus laudare, eosdem reddit inimicos metus. (207)

Vocabulary: *cogit*: [T.1]
is-dem, ea-dem, id-dem: the same [analyze *eos* for the gender, number, and function of this word]
reddere: [T.1] to render

at qui favoris gloriam veri petit, animo magis quam voce laudari volet. (209)

Vocabulary: [difference between *at* and *et*??]
favoris . . . veri: of true favor
petit: [T.1]
animo . . . voce . . . : with the heart . . . with the voice
magis quam: more than
laudari: to be praised
volet (*volo, velle . . .*): [T.3]

modo inter illa, quae putant cuncti aspera, fortis fui laetusque. (417)

Vocabulary: *modo*: recently, just now
ille, illa, illud [think Block 1 endings]: that

1. What rule applies to adjectives standing on their own in a sentence (Lesson 5)?

2. Say in Latin: "Among those men, whom all we women consider rough, you [pl] had been happy."

Causam timoris ipse quam ignoro exigis. (434)

Vocabulary: *timoris*: of a fear
ipse: I myself [push *ipse* back inside the relative box!]
exigere: [T.1] demand, require

quem dies vidit veniens superbum, hunc dies vidit fugiens iacentem. (613)

Vocabulary: *veniens* (subject): arriving, breaking
hunc (m object): this
fugiens (subject): fleeing, departing
iacentem (sing object): lying prostrate, in ruins

Aries praeceps ibit in undas, per quas pavidam vexerat Hellen. (850)

Vocabulary: *Aries* (subject): the ram
praeceps (subject): headlong
eo, ire: [T.3]
vexerat: [*vehere*]
Hellen (object): Helle

1. Give six possible translations of *in* when followed by the object function.

2. Say in Latin: "The examples [*exemplum*], through which we will have carried our minds [*animus*], have helped [*adiuvare*] us."

Post-Classical Latin Translation Practice

Liturgia Romana, Paulus VI (1897–1978 PC)

These readings and prayers are taken from the *Liturgy of the Hours*, "Commune Sanctarum Mulierum." In each case, identify the relative pronoun and the verb that goes with it. Think about the relative "box" or clause. Where it is not translated for you, find the main verb and translate the main clause first.

Quae mihi erant lucra, haec arbitratus sum propter Christum detrimentum.

Lectio brevis, Phil 3.7–8

Vocabulary: *mihi*: to me
haec (object): these things
arbitratus sum: I have judged

1. Find another preposition with the same meaning as *propter* (consult Lesson 6).

Preces

Per viduas, quae oratione et hospitalitate solitudinem suam levaverunt ac sanctificaverunt, . . .

Vocabulary: *oratione . . . hospitalitate*: through prayer . . . through hospitality
solitudinem (object): solitude

–da Ecclesiae tuae sacramentum caritatis tuae mundo exhibere.

—grant it to your Church to reveal the sacrament of your love to the world.

Per matres, quae prolem ad regnum Dei et ad consortium humanum genuerunt, . . .

Vocabulary: *prolem* (object): offspring

—da Ecclesiae tuae, ut homines universos ad vitam generet atque salutem.

—grant it to your Church, that it might bring forth all people to life and salvation.

PRECES

Domine Iesu, magister, quem Maria audiebat, cum Martha tibi serviebat, . . .

Vocabulary: *cum*: when
tibi: to you
servire: [T.2] to be of service

—concede nobis, ut in fide et caritate serviamus tibi.

—grant to us, that we might be of service to you in faith and love.

Lectio brevis Gal 6.7b–8

Quae seminaverit homo, haec et metet; quoniam, qui seminat in carne sua, de carne metet corruptionem, qui autem seminat in spiritu, de spiritu metet vitam aeternam.

Vocabulary: *seminare*: to sow [*seminat* = T.1]
homo (subject): a man, person
metet: [T.3]
in / de carne sua: in / from his flesh
corruptionem (object): corruption
in / de spiritu: in / from the spirit

1. What else can *et* mean, if it doesn't mean "and"?

V/. Inveni quem diligit anima mea. R/. Tenui eum, nec dimittam.

Vocabulary: *diligit*: [T.1]
dimittam: [T.3]

1. What pronoun is "omitted" from the first half of this sentence?

Lectio brevis, Rom 8.28–30

quos autem praedestinavit, hos et vocavit; et quos vocavit, hos et iustificavit; quos autem iustificavit, illos et glorificavit.

Vocabulary: *hos ... illos* (m object pl): these men ... those men

1. Give the T.5 and T.6 forms for all the verbs in the text, keeping the subject the same.

LESSON 12

THE REMAINING VERB TIMES

There are four main groups of verbs; each group has a theme vowel (see chart below). Any irregularities or omitted principal parts will be indicated by the dictionary. Where principal parts are completely regular, for example as often happens with Group 1 verbs, they will not be given by the dictionary. The dictionary may simply denote the group with a number in brackets: *dubito* (1). Sample principal parts are as follows:

Group 1 (40%)	[pretty regular]	**paro, parare, paravi, paratus -a -um**	*prepare*
Group 2 (10%)	[quite irregular]	**habeo, habere, habui, habitus -a -um**	*have*
		maneo, manere, mansi, mansus -a -um	*remain*
Group 3 (40%)	[totally irregular]	**dico, dicere, dixi, dictus -a -um**	*say*
Group 4 (10%)	[pretty regular]	**audio, audire, audivi, auditus -a -um**	*hear*

To put a verb in the right group you have to look at PP1 and PP2:

Group and Theme Vowel	*PP1 ends in*	*PP2 ends in*
Group 1: a	-o	-are
Group 2: strong e	-eo	-ere
Group 3: weak e	-o	-ere
Group 4: i	-io	-ire
Fence/mixed verbs	-io	-ere

A Note on Fence Verbs

There are a handful of verbs (about ten, and numerous compounds of the same; e.g., *perficio, efficio, deficio, afficio, eripio, deripio,* etc.) that don't fit perfectly into Group 1, 2, 3, or 4. Their principal parts look like this:

rapio, rapere, rapui, raptus -a -um	*snatch*
facio, facere, feci, factus -a -um	*make, do*

You will see that PP1 looks as if the verb belongs to Group 4, but PP2 looks as if the verb belongs to Group 3. These are "fence" verbs, because they stand on the fence between Groups 3 and 4. **With one or two exceptions, treat fence verbs as if they belong to Group 4, even though in the dictionary they are labeled as Group 3.**

Identifying Times 1-2-3

PP1 is the stem for Times 1-2-3.

In order to identify and form Times 1-2-3 you need to know which "group" a verb belongs to. You use the theme vowel in a certain way each time. These times are not quite as simple as T.4-5-6, though there are patterns. Exceptions to the patterns are indicated below in italics. Whatever time you are reading, the person doing the verb is always recognized in the ending on the verb: **o-m-i / s-sti**/ t / mus / tis-stis** / nt-erunt**.**

Once you see the pattern, fill in the gaps in the charts below:

Time 1: Present Tense

Pattern: PP1 + theme vowel + person endings (pattern breakers in *italics*)

Group 1 (-o, -are)	*Group 2 (-eo, -ere)*	*Group 3 (-o, -ere)*	*Group 4 (-io, -ire) / Fence (-io, -ere)*
amo	moneo	dico	*audio*
amas	mones	dic*i*s	
amat	monet		
amamus			audimus
amatis		dic*i*tis	auditis
amant		dic*u*nt	audi*u*nt

Time 2: Imperfect Tense

Pattern: PP1 + theme vowel + *-ba-* + person endings

Group 1 (-o, -are)	*Group 2 (-eo, -ere)*	*Group 3 (-o, -ere)*	*Group 4 (-io, -ire) / Fence (-io, -ere)*
amabam	monebam	dicebam	audi*e*bam
amabas	monebas	dicebas	audi*e*bas

Time 3: Future Tense

Pattern for Group 1 and 2: PP1 + theme vowel + *-bo -bis -bit -bimus -bitis -bunt*

Pattern for Group 3, 4, and fence: PP1 + *-am -es -et -emus -etis -ent*

Group 1 (-o, -are)	*Group 2 (-eo, -ere)*	*Group 3 (-o, -ere)*	*Group 4 (-io, -ire) / Fence (-io, -ere)*
amabo	**monebo**	**dicam**	**audiam**
amabis	**monebis**	**dices**	**audies**
amabit	________	________	**audiet**
amabimus	________	________	________
amabitis	________	**dicetis**	________
amabunt	________	**dicent**	________

Difficulties of Time 3

Given the importance of the theme vowel, especially given the two patterns for Time 3, it is essential to know where a verb comes from in the dictionary. Otherwise, you will fall into bad traps! Carefully translate the following verb forms, the first example in each group is done for you:

a. *ducebam* I was leading
i. *vertam* ________________

b. *paras* you prepare
i. *currebas* ________________
ii. *audiveras* ________________

c. *monet* he/she/it warns
i. *ducet* ________________

d. *audis* you hear
i. *moveris* ________________
ii. *movebis* ________________
iii. *eris* ________________

Translation Tips

You now know how to form and recognize all six indicative times. When you are reading a Latin sentence, there are some steps you can go through that will lead you to identify which verb time it is more quickly and accurately.

Focus verb: **facio, facere, feci, factus** *do*

1. Is the stem for the verb PP1 or PP3? From the verb above, does my verb form begin *fac-* or *fec-*? This will cut your available options by fifty percent.
2. If the stem for the verb is PP1 (*fac-*), the possible times are T.1-2-3. If the stem for the verb is PP3 (*fec-*), the possible times are T.4-5-6.
3. If the stem for the verb is PP1 (*fac-*), ask yourself if the verb form contains the letters **ba**. If it does, you are looking at T.2. If it does not, you are looking at T.1 or T.3. To differentiate between T.1 and T.3 you really will need to check the group of the verb in the dictionary. Remember that for T.3, Groups 1 and 2 end in -**bo, -bis, -bit, -bimus, -bitis, -bunt**; for Groups 3, 4 and fence, the endings will be **-am, -es, -et, -emus, -etis, -ent**.
4. If the stem for the verb is PP3 (*fec-*), look for the simple differences between T.4-5-6. T.4 has the **special endings and mostly contains **i**. T.5 ("had") contains **era**. T.6 ("will have") contains **eri**.
5. Regardless of verb time, the ending on the verb will always tell you who is doing the verb.
6. Identify the time of the following verbs, then translate them with all available meanings suggested in Lesson 7.

faciebatis ________________________________

fecimus ________________________________

faciam ________________________________

feceris ________________________________

facit ________________________________

fecerant ________________________________

Sometimes PP1 and PP3 have the same stem. This means it can be hard to tell the difference between T.1 and T.4, resulting in up to seven different possible meanings for one verb form (see Lesson 7):

attendit

contendimus

venit

Classical Latin Translation Practice

Publius Ovidius Naso (43 AC–c. 18 PC)

ludunt formosae; casta est, quam nemo rogavit—
aut, si rusticitas non vetat, ipsa rogat.

Amores 1.8.43–44

Vocabulary: *ludere*: to play around
rogare: to proposition
rusticitas (subject): lack of sophistication
ipsa (subject): she herself

1. Which verb connects with *quam*? Who, or what, is its antecedent?

2. Focus on the new verb times in the text and give translations for *ludunt*, *vetat*, and *rogat*. Give the T.2 and T.3 forms for these verbs, keeping the subject the same.

ante mare et terras et quod tegit omnia caelum
unus erat toto naturae vultus in orbe,
quem dixere Chaos.

Metamorphoses 1.5–7

Vocabulary: *omnia*: (n pl object): all things
toto in orbe: in the whole world

1. Look up *mare* in the dictionary. How can we be confident from its gender that this strange looking form can be an object after *ante*? Explain.

2. What verb links with *quod*? What time is this verb? What is the antecedent of *quod*, bearing in mind Lesson 11, principle 2.

3. From the word *natura, naturae* (f): "nature," what is the function and meaning of *naturae*, if it is *not* subject plural? (Lesson 2)

4. What is the word *dixere* a shortened form of? (Lesson 8)

5. What is the antecedent of *quem*?

Ut fugiant aquilas, timidissima turba, columbae,
Ut fugit invisos agna novella lupos:
Sic illae timuere viros sine more ruentes;
Constitit in nulla qui fuit ante color.

Ars Amatoria 1.117–120

Vocabulary:
ut: just as
timidissimus -a -um: extremely timid
ille, illa, illud; that
timuere (*timeo, timere*): [a shortened form of which verb time?]
sine more: without restraint
ruentes (object pl): rushing
constare: to remain, abide
in nulla: in no woman

1. Identify the time you see in *fugiunt* and *fugit*. Check the principal parts and identify what special group this verb belongs to. Give the other five verb times for both subjects.

2. Think carefully and identify the antecedent of *qui*.

Post-Classical Latin Translation Practice

Biblia Vulgata, Hieronymus (347–420 PC)

Qui invenit animam suam, perdet illam: et qui perdiderit animam suam propter me, inveniet eam.
Qui recipit vos, me recipit: et qui me recipit, recipit eum, qui me misit.

Evangelium Secundum Matthaeum
10.39–40

1. Identify the *omitted* antecedent of *qui*. Identify in each sentence which verb belongs with *qui* and which verb is the main verb.

2. What is difficult about identifying the verb time of *invenit*?

3. Identify the time of *perdet* and *inveniet*. Why is identifying verb group especially important for this time? Explain.

Carmina Burana (thirteenth century PC)

In taberna quando sumus,
non curamus quid sit humus.

"In taberna quando sumus" 196

Vocabulary: *humus -i* (f): ground, tomb
quid sit: what is

1. Write in Latin:

a. "When they will have been in the pub we will not care"

b. "When you (sing) used to be in the pub they used to care"

c. "When he has been in the pub she cares"

Bibit pauper et aegrotus,
bibit exul et ignotus,
bibit puer, bibit canus,
bibit praesul et decanus,
bibit soror, bibit frater,
bibit anus, bibit mater,
bibit ista, bibit ille,
bibunt centum, bibunt mille.

Vocabulary: *anus -us* (f): old woman
ista: that woman
ille: that man

1. Check the dictionary and write out in full all the principal parts of the verb *bibo*. Give the exact meaning of each principal part. What seven possible translations are there for the form of the verb *bibit*? Which time do you think *bibit* is here, given the form *bibunt*?

2. What must you do when you read an adjective on its own in a Latin sentence? Therefore, give the full meaning of *pauper* and *aegrotus*.

3. What is the full meaning of *canus*? (Don't assume it means "dog"!!) Write in Latin using only five words: "The gray-haired dog sings [*cano, canere*] gray-haired things and gray-haired women."

4. Write in Latin:

   a. "I, a poor man, will have drunk"

   b. "We sick people had drunk"

   c. "Children have drunk"

   d. "You old woman will drink"

   e. "I, a gray-haired old woman, was drinking pure [*merus -a -um*] wines [*vinum -i* (n)], just as [*sicut*] you [pl] sick people will drink them before me and my [*meus -a -um*] colleagues [*collega -ae* (c)]."

LUDUS 4

AFTER LESSONS 10–12

Topics covered: *the relative pronoun; verb groups; T.1-2-3.*

To start, write in Latin the following phrases of William Shakespeare (1564–1616 PC).

A.

"For he will never follow anything that other men begin."

Julius Caesar 1.3.151

Vocabulary: follow: *repeto, repetere, repetivi, repetitum*
anything that = that which
other: *alius, alia, aliud*
begin: *incoho, incohare, incohavi, incohatum*

1. Now modify your Latin by using principles two and three (Lesson 11).

2. Now modify the verbs to read: "he will never have repeated … will have begun."

B.

"I am no orator, as Brutus is, but—as you know me all—a plain, blunt man that love my friend."

Julius Caesar 3.2.220

Vocabulary: as: *sicut, velut, ut*
know: *cognosco, cognoscere, cognovi, cognitum*
plain: *simplex*
blunt: *apertus -a -um*
that = who [Begin with relative clause.]

C.

Around the time of Julius Caesar in Rome (60–30 AC), a stage actor from Syria, Publilius Syrus, became the author of seven hundred or more one-line bits of wisdom and insight. Here are some. I warn you: they are more subtle and meaningful than you may think on first sight!

qui omnes insidias timet in nullas incidit. (*Sententiae* 594)

Vocabulary: *insidia -ae* (f): plot, trap, ambush

1. If the verb is *timeo, timere*: fear, then it belongs to which group?

2. What time is *timet*?

3. If the verb is *incido, incidere*: fall, then it belongs to which group?

4. What time is *incidit*?

5. Give the "they" forms for those verbs in Times 1, 2 and 3.

6. What gender do you see in *insidias … nullas*?

7. Therefore, how can you explain fully the gender you see in *qui*?

8. Which verb connects with *qui*?

9. What is the main verb in the sentence?

10. Translate the line.

D.

Bona mors est homini vitae quae exstinguit mala. (*Sententiae* 67)

Vocabulary: *mors* (subject): death
homini: for a person

1. From the word *vitae -ae* (f): life, what function-case must *vitae* in the text be?

2. Think carefully and point out the gender of the following words (any error here destroys everything!): *mors, bona, mala.*

3. Check your dictionary for the verb *exstinguo* and then give the other five indicative times in Latin and English, with the same subject as in the line above, indicating the T. number.

4. Translate the line.

5. What do these sayings mean?

a. *mala inter nos es quae bona inter eos facis.*

b. *bona cantas quam audimus.*

c. *mala inter eos eris quae mala inter nos manseris.*

d. *bona cantas quae audimus.*

E.

Facit <u>gradum</u> <u>Fortuna</u> quem nemo videt. (*Sententiae* 221)

Vocabulary: *gradus* (m): step, pace
Fortuna (f): Goddess of Luck, Fortune

1. Translate the line.

2. What does "*facit gradum Fortuna quam nemo videt*" mean?

3. Check the dictionary for the PPs of the two verbs given in the text and give the T.4 form, keeping the subject the same. Note how one letter in Latin makes all the difference.

F.

Fortuna <u>nimium</u> quem fovet stultum facit. (*Sententiae* 203)

Vocabulary: *nimium*: too much, excessively

1. From our principle about relative boxes, what is the main verb here? Its subject?

2. With which verb does *quem* connect? What function-case is *quem*?

3. With what does the adjective *stultum* agree? (A million superficial Latinists are going to fail when asked. You will succeed....)

4. And so, what is the antecedent of *quem*? (subtle stuff)

5. How in Latin can verbs like *fovet* and *facit* possibly be the same Time? Explain fully.

6. If the verb *fovere* means to cherish, translate the line:

7. Reverse every word except *nimium* (an adverb).

8. What do these Publilius-inspired sayings mean?

a. *fortunam nimium qui fovent stulta faciunt.*

b. *fortuna nimium quae fovent stulti stulta facit.*

G.

Negat sibi ipse qui quod difficile est petit. (*Sententiae* 460)

Vocabulary: *sibi*: himself
ipse: he
difficile (n sing): difficult

1. To what groups do the verbs here belong?

2. Give the T.2 forms of those verbs with "I" as the subject.

3. According to our relative box principle, what is the verb for *qui*? for *quod*?

4. *Sibi*, *ipse*, and *qui* are all masculine. What gender is *quod*?

5. What is the antecedent of *quod*? Can you see it?

6. As what does that antecedent function in its own clause? (Answering these questions with precision is difficult but essential in Latin.)

7. Translate the line.

8. Expressing all pronouns, write in Latin in six words, "We shall be denying those things which you will have sought."

9. Now reduce that sentence to three essential words.

H.

Quod aetas vitium posuit aetas auferet. (*Sententiae* 566)

Vocabulary: *vitium -i* (n): fault, defect
aetas (subject): age
pono, ponere: put, place
aufero, auferre: take away

1. Translate the consoling line.

2. Reverse the line (*aetas* becomes *aetates*).

LESSON 13

BLOCK 2 NOUNS

As we learned in Lesson 2, 40% of all Latin nouns belong to Block 1. Likewise, 40% of all Latin nouns belong to Block 2. Words belonging to Block 2 all have the same endings, which change according to what function the word has in the sentence, and according to the noun's number (whether it is singular or plural). You can identify whether a noun belongs to this family by how it appears in the dictionary:

1	*2*	*3*	*4*
crazy form	*-is*	*(m/f/n)*	*meaning*
homo,	**hominis**	**(m)**	a man
lex,	**legis**	**(f)**	a law
corpus,	**corporis**	**(n)**	a body

As with Block 1 nouns, in each case the dictionary entry gives you four pieces of information:

1. the noun in **subject singular** (the first form we call "crazy" because each looks different, and it is a crazy, unpredictable form);
2. the **of-possession (genitive) singular**, which is the sign of which block the noun belongs to (**an of-possession [genitive] singular ending in *is* is the sign of Block 2**);
3. the grammatical gender of the noun (masculine, feminine, or neuter);
4. the meaning of the noun.

Notes

- The second form (if you take away the *-is*) gives you the stem for the endings. **Do not put endings on the crazy form.**
- There is no distinction between masculine, feminine, and neuter in the way the words appear or in their endings, except for the familiar neuter super rules.
- It can be very hard to find the subject (crazy) form in the dictionary, if you are not looking at the crazy part in the text you are reading. This may be the work of many afternoons …

The 80/20 Rule

Because of the stem of some Block 2 words, sometimes there are alternative endings: 80% of Block 2 neuter plural nouns end in *-a*, 20% of them end in *-ia*. The proportions are the other way round for adjectives: 80% of Block 2 neuter adjectives end in *-ia*, and 20% in *-a*. We will refer to this variation as the 80/20 rule.

The more you read, the more you'll get to know which nouns and adjectives have the rarer 20% ending.

Nouns that appear like this in the dictionary change their endings in the following way:

	M & F	*N*
subject singular	**crazy**	**crazy**
subject plural	**-es**	**-a / -ia** 80 / 20
object singular	**-em**	**crazy**
object plural	**-es**	**-a / -ia** 80 / 20

Notes

- Note that masculine and feminine subject and object plurals look the same. This will lend some interest to your reading!

  oves pastores servaverunt

Here, common sense suggests that *pastores* is the subject and *oves* the object, since the verb *servare* means to protect.

fratres sorores vident.

- This sentence is entirely ambiguous, and whether the brothers see the sisters or the sisters see the brothers, not even the angels could tell you!
- The singular object *-em* ending is sometimes written *-im*. For example, the object of *vis* (strength) is *vim*, not *vem*. The object of *navis* (ship) is found as both *navem* and *navim*. These are common variations you will come across in your reading. Also, the plural object form *-es* (and occasionally the subject plural) is commonly written *-is*: *naves* and *navis*. The *i* in this ending is long in quantity, a concept we will pick up in the advanced workbook.

Become accustomed to very long dictionary forms in Block 2: be prepared to string the whole word out:

pulchritudo, pulchritudinis (f), beauty

(This tells you that the word becomes *pulchritudin-es* NOT *pulchritud-es*. **Never put endings on the crazy form!!**)

- You will get used to patterns of Block 2 nouns: for instance, abstract qualities are often feminine nouns ending in *-as*: *dignitas, dignitatis* (f), dignity, worth

  Stay aware of block and gender. Do not make assumptions about a word, but get to know the whole dictionary entry. The dictionary is your bible.

Find the following words in the dictionary, and give the subject plural form, according to block and gender:

virtus ______________________________

corpus ______________________________

amicus ______________________________

Classical Latin Translation Practice

Titus Maccius Plautus (254–184 AC)

itaque inter se commutant vestem et nomina. (*Captivi*, Prologus 37)

Vocabulary: *se*: themselves

auctio fiet. . . . venibunt servi, supellex, fundi et aedes, omnia. . . .
venibit uxor quoque etiam, si quis emptor venerit.

Menaechmi 1157–1160

Vocabulary: *fieri*: to be held [T.3]
quis (subject): any

1. Scrutinize your dictionary and point out the difference in meaning between *venio, venire* and *veneo, venire* (*venum-eo*). Write out the principal parts for each verb.

2. What time must *veni-bunt* and *veni-bit* be? Meaning?

3. And, bearing in mind the principal parts, what is the meaning of *venerit*?

4. What are the five Block 2 nouns in the text above? Reverse each one.

5. Write in Latin: "Wives will also be sold, if I will have found buyers."

Publius Terentius Afer (185–159 AC)

fores effregit atque in aedis inruit
alienas; ipsum dominum atque omnem familiam
mulcavit usque ad mortem; eripuit mulierem
quam amabat.

Adelphoe 88–91

Vocabulary: *foris, foris* (f): a door
inruit (see *irruo*): invade, rush into
ipsum (object): himself
usque: right up, all the way

1. Look back at the notes to this lesson and explain how *aedis* can be in the object function after the preposition *in*. What adjective must be agreeing with *aedis*?

2. In the last part of the sentence, which verb goes with *quam* and which is the main verb?

3. Write in Latin: "We will snatch away the women whom they will have loved!"

Post-Classical Latin Translation Practice

Liturgia Romana, Paulus VI (1897–1978 PC)

Quadragesima—the fortieth day before Easter, Die Cinerum

Deus, qui non mortem, sed conversionem desideras peccatorum: fragilitatem condicionis humanæ ... respice; et hos cineres, quos ... capitibus nostris imponi decernimus, benedicere pro tua pietate dignare.

Vocabulary: *peccatorum*: of sinners
respice [command]: look upon!
hos (object pl): these
capitibus nostris: on our heads
imponi: to be placed
dignare [command]: deign! condescend!
pro: according to

1. Look up the following Block 2 nouns in the dictionary and in each instance identify the function and number you see in the text: *mors, conversio, fragilitas, condicio, cinis.*

2. What important features of Block 2 nouns do these nouns demonstrate?

3. What determines the gender and number of *qui* and *quos*? What determines their function? Point out the antecedent of these relative pronouns.

4. If the verbs are *desiderare*, "to wish" and *decernere*, "to decide," then what time do you see in the text? Give the T.2 forms, keeping the subjects the same.

5. What essential principle of Latin word order did you learn in conjunction with relative pronouns (see Lesson 11)? Which verbs are the main verbs in this text, therefore?

6. Using the relative pronoun principles from Lesson 11, say elegantly in Latin: "We women, who are desiring not death but conversion, have decided to learn the language, which peoples [*populus -i* (m)] have used [*adhibere*] through innumerable [*innumerus -a -um*] centuries [*saeculum -i* (n)]."

Petrus Chrysologus (400–450 PC)

Si Dominum fugitis, quare non recurritis ad parentem? ... venite ergo, redite et vel sic probate patrem, quem videtis pro malis bona, pro iniuriis amorem, pro vulneribus tantis tantam reddere caritatem ... / ... fratres, hoc sacrificium Christi descendit ex forma qui corpus suum pro vita saeculi vitaliter immolavit; et vere corpus suum fecit hostiam vivam, quia vivit occisus.... Deus fidem non mortem quaerit; votum non sanguinem sitit.

Sermo 108

Vocabulary:
quare: why, for what reason
vel: even
venite, redite, probate [all commands]: come! return! approve!
pro: instead of
quem ... reddere: whom ... to give back
ex forma: from the form-nature
saeculi: of the world
votum -i (n): prayer

1. Hunt in the dictionary and find the root words—crazy forms for *parentem, patrem, amorem, caritatem, fratrem, fidem, mortem.* Reverse each one.

2. What verb times do you variously identify in the verbs *fugitis*, *recurritis*, *videtis*, *immolavit*, *fecit*, *vivit*, *quaerit*, and *sitit*? Reverse each one and then give the T.3 form for each verb, keeping the subjects the same.

3. From the verb *occidere* (to kill), what is the full meaning of PP4 *occisus*?

4. Say in Latin: "They sacrificed their bodies."

BLOCK 2 ADJECTIVES

Block 2 adjectives account for 50 percent of all adjectives in Latin (the other 50 percent are Block 1). They are slightly tricky because they appear in the dictionary in three different ways.

Type	*Dictionary Entry*	*Dictionary Entry Explained*
Type 1 one gender option	M/F/N **audax, audacis** *bold*	M/F/N subject singular (crazy), genitive singular (*-is*) Works just like Block 2 nouns. Take off the *-is* for the stem for the endings.
Type 2 two gender options **(this form is most common)**	M/F N **insignis, insigne** *distinguished, remarkable*	M & F subject singular, N subject/object singular Take off the *-is* for the stem for the endings.
Type 3 three gender options	M F N **acer, acris, acre** *sharp, fierce*	M subject singular, F subj sing, N subject/object singular Take off the *-is* for the stem for the endings.

The one to watch out for and remember is the neuter subject/object singular form ending in *-e*. This is nasty, as it does not look like a subject/object ending: Learn this properly now to protect yourself from future confusion with ablatives and adverbs!

acre verbum dixit

he/she/it spoke a sharp word

Block 2 adjectives have the same endings as Block 2 nouns. The only variation is that the neuter subject and object plural ending for adjectives is -*ia* (80%) and -*a* (20%)—the reverse of Block 2 nouns. Always put the endings on the stem provided by taking off -*is*. Never touch the crazy form!

puellae acria et audacia sunt verba

the words of the girl are sharp and bold

Look up the following common Latin adjectives, and note down how they are presented in the dictionary and which block they are. If Block 2, identify type (one, two, or three gender options):

omnis ______________________________

piger ______________________________

celer ______________________________

ferox ______________________________

brevis ______________________________

uber ______________________________

vetus ______________________________

blandus ______________________________

facilis ______________________________

miser ______________________________

Combining Block 1 and Block 2

It's really important that you get to know how nouns and adjectives appear in the dictionary and put them in the right Block. Once that is straight, it is *really* important you keep them in the right block and apply the right endings. A Block 1 adjective may be used to describe a Block 2 noun, but a Block 1 adjective will never have a Block 2 ending on it. A Block 2 adjective may be used to describe a Block 1 noun, but a Block 2 adjective will never have a Block 1 ending on it.

prudens, prudentis:	*wise*
prudens vir	*a wise man*
prudens femina	*a wise woman*
prudens verbum	*a wise word*

• Reverse the three phrases above.

Now, using the correct form of the verb *audire*, write in Latin:

We used to hear the wise men.

They will hear the wise women.

I will have heard the wise words.

Big Prose Composition Practice

Because-of [preposition] a wish [*cupiditas*] having-been-expressed [*exprimo*] we shall now be reading [both *lego* and *lectito*] the Latin works [*opus*], which smart [*eruditus*; *doctus*] women [*mulier*] wrote before long [*longus*] ages [*aetas*] (=a long time ago), while [*dum* or *cum*] the other [*reliquus*] individuals [*homo*] around [preposition] us are sleeping [*dormio*] and yawning [*oscitare*] and moving [*movere*] their [*suus -a -um*] toys [*crepundia* (n pl)] and gifts [*munus*] around [preposition] the wide [*latus*] beaches [*litus*].

Classical Latin Translation Practice

Sulpicia (c. 40 AC), niece and ward of M. Valerius Messalla Corvinus (64 AC–8 PC)

Invisus natalis adest, qui rure molesto
et sine Cerintho tristis agendus erit.

Poem 2

Vocabulary: *natalis -is* (m): a birthday
rure molesto: in the annoying countryside
sine Cerintho: without Cerinthus
agendus -a -um: needing to be spent

1. How does Sulpicia describe her birthday in the main clause?

2. The relative clause explains why and describes the birthday with which other adjective?

3. What is the verb time of *erit*?

4. Reverse the entire two lines, omitting *rure molesto* and *sine Cerintho.*

Estne tibi, Cerinthe, tuae pia cura puellae,
quod mea nunc vexat corpora fessa calor?
A! ego non aliter tristes evincere morbos
optarim, quam te si quoque velle putem.

Poem 5

Vocabulary: *ne*: turns a statement into a question
tibi: to you
tuae puellae: for your girlfriend
non aliter . . . quam si . . . : in no other way . . . than if
optarim: would I wish
putem: I thought

1. What strange-looking noun is the subject of *vexat*? What is its gender? Reverse line 2, omitting *quod* and *nunc*.

2. Look up the principal parts of the verb *evinco*, and give the meaning of *evincere*.

3. Look up the principal parts of the verb *volo*, and give the meaning of *velle*.

hesterna . . . te solum . . . nocte reliqui,
ardorem cupiens dissimulare meum.

Poem 6

Vocabulary: *hesterna nocte*: last night
cupiens, cupientis: desiring

1. Write in Latin: "We had left you-women alone, desiring to conceal our ardors!"

Titus Lucretius Carus (c. 99–c. 55 AC)

"Iam iam non domus accipiet te laeta neque uxor
optima, nec dulces occurrent oscula nati
praeripere et tacita pectus dulcedine tangent."

De Rerum Natura 3.894–96

Vocabulary: *domus* (f): home
optimus -a -um: excellent, best
natus -i (m): son, child
tacita . . . dulcedine: with silent sweetness

1. Look up and write out the principal parts of *accipio*. To what special group of verbs does it belong? What verb time do you identify in *accipiet*? Give the *ego* form for that time.

---

2. Which adjective goes with *nati*?

---

3. Which noun is the object of the infinitive *praeripere*?

---

4. How is it possible for a noun ending in *-us* like *pectus* to be an object?

Post-Classical Latin Translation Practice

Hrotsvitha Gandeshemensis (c. 935–c. 1002 PC)

{Agapes} Quid facit?
{Hirena} Nunc ollas <u>molli</u> fovet <u>gremio</u>, nunc sartagines et <u>caccabos amplectitur</u>, <u>mitia</u> <u>libans</u> oscula.
{Chionia} Ridiculum.

Dulcitius, Scene 4

Vocabulary: *molli gremio*: in his unmanly lap
caccabus -i (m): saucepan, cauldron
amplectitur: he embraces
mitis, mite: soft
libans, libantis: pouring out, offering

1. Take the time to find the subject form of *sartagines* in the dictionary. To which block of nouns does this belong? Why was the plural form *sartagines* and not *sartages*. Explain fully, using the notes to Lesson 13.

___

___

2. Give the reverse form of *mitia oscula*.

___

{Hirena} Voluptas parit poenam, necessitas autem coronam; nec dicitur reatus, nisi quod consentit animus.

Dulcitius, Scene 12

Vocabulary: *dicitur reatus*: a person is proclaimed guilty

1. Write in Latin: "Your [pl] pleasures produced punishments, but our compulsions had produced crowns because our minds were consenting."

Hildegardis Abbatissa (1098–1179 PC)

Ipse etiam Deus virum fortem et feminam debilem creaverat, cuius debilitas mundum generavit. Et divinitas fortis est, caro autem filii Dei infirma, per quam mundus in priorem vitam recuperatur.

Liber vitae meritorum P.IV.32

Vocabulary: *ipse* (subject): himself
cuius: whose
prior, prioris: former
recuperatur: is recovered

1. Keeping the subject the same, give the other five times of *creaverat* and their translations.

2. Say in Latin: "I will have generated strong men and the weak women, because [*quod*] my [*meus -a -um*] flesh is weak [use *debilis -e* and *infirmus -a -um*]."

Reginaldus Foster (1939–2020 PC)

omnES divES vidES milES opES penES principES divitES. PauperES inveniES civES penES potentES latronES, legES legES regES regES numquam.

Ludorum Domesticorum Ridicula

1. What problem about Latin do these nonsense sentences demonstrate?

2. What rules set out in Lesson 1 and Lesson 6 should you follow to unravel the meaning of a Latin sentence?

LESSON 15

TWO WAYS OF EXPRESSING COMMANDS

To express a command you use the imperative mood. This can be expressed in two ways.

Type A: The Present Imperative (Normal)

Commanding	*Group 1*	*Group 2*	*Group 3*	*Group 4*
tu *you*	**ama!** *love!*	**tace!**	**scribe!**	**audi!**
vos *y'all*	**amate!** *love!*	**tacete!**	**scrib*i*te!**	**audite!**

To form the first type of imperative,

- Take PP1 and remove the *-o*.
- For singular, add the theme vowel, for plural, add the theme vowel plus *-te* (notice the Group 3 exception in the chart above).
- Notice how the theme vowel plays a part in the forms.
- **Treat Fence verbs as Group 3.**

Type B: The Future / Legal / Comic / Biblical Imperative

Commanding	*Group 1*	*Group 2*	*Group 3*	*Group 4*
tu (you) **is/ea/id** (he/she/it)	**amato!** *love!* *you shall love!* *he/she/it shall love!* *let him love!*	**taceto!**	**scribito!**	**audito!**
vos (you [pl])	**amatote!** *love!* *you shall love!*	**tacetote!**	**scribitote!**	**auditote!**
ei/eae/ea (they)	**amanto!** *they shall love!* *let them love!*	**tacento!**	**scribunto!**	**audiunto!**

To form the second type of imperative,

- For the singular imperative, take the T.1 he/she/it form and add *-o*.
- When commanding "you plural", take the T.1 he/she/it form and add *-ote*.
- When commanding "they," take the T.1 they form and add *-o*.

The Imperative of the Verb "To Be"

A: **es!**
este!

B: **esto!**
estote!
sunto!

Expressing Negative Commands

The negative for the indicative is *non* (not) or *nec* (nor).

The negative for all commands is *ne*. This is because commands are imperative and not indicative.

ne audi! ne audito!	*don't listen!*

You can also express negative direct commands using the imperative of *nolo* (I do not want) followed by PP2 of any verb. This has the same meaning as *ne* + imperative: *don't . . . !*

noli audire!	*don't listen!*
nolite abire!	*don't go away!*

Examples

cras petito, nunc abi!
Ask tomorrow; now go away!

salus populi suprema lex esto.
The safety of the people shall be the supreme law.

Classical Latin Translation Practice

More brilliant one-liners from our beloved Marcus Tullius Cicero (106–43 AC).

valete, mea desideria, valete. (*Ad Familiares* 14.2)

1. Reverse the whole sentence.

cura te, si me amas, diligenter. (*Ad Familiares* 16.20)

1. Reverse the whole sentence, apart from *si* and *diligenter.*

tu ista omnia vide et guberna. (*Ad Atticum* 3.8)

1. From the adjective *omnis, omne*, what must *omnia* mean on its own in the sentence?

2. Give the "B Type," or legal / future form, of the imperatives used here.

totum investiga, cognosce, perspice et illum nebulonem ... ex istis locis amove. (*Ad Atticum* 1.12)

Vocabulary: *ex istis locis*: from that neighborhood

1. Assuming for now that the word *ille, illa, illud* inflects rather like Block 1, give the reverse forms for *illum nebulonem*.

si <u>rem nullam</u> habebis, quod in buccam venerit scribito. (*Ad Atticum* 1.12)

Vocabulary: *rem nullam* (object): no subject matter

1. Think hard, remembering the principles from Lesson 11, and give the omitted Latin pronoun, which must be the antecedent of that *quod*, and object of *scribito*.

Gaius Plinius Secundus (23–79 PC)

in <u>hunc</u> ponito arbores vitesque. sed <u>hoc flante</u> ne arato, frugem ne serito, semen ne iacito.

Naturalis Historia 18.116

Vocabulary: *hunc* = *ventum aquilonem*: the north wind, Boreas
hoc flante: while this is blowing

1. How else might Pliny have expressed the negative imperatives here? Give two different options.

Lex Duodecim Tabularum (451–450 AC)

[1] **hominem mortuum in urbe ne sepelito neve urito.** (10)

Vocabulary: *-ve*: or

1. Give the reverse forms for *hominem mortuum.*

[2] **si pater filium ter venumduit, filius a patre liber esto.** (4)

Vocabulary: *ter*: three times
venumdare: sell
a patre: from the father [Time 4]

1. Say in Latin: "If the fathers have sold the sons, let the sons be free!"

Post-Classical Latin Translation Practice

Liturgia Romana, Paulus VI (1897–1978 PC)

Veni, Sancte Spiritus,
et *emitte* caelitus
lucis tuae radium.
Veni, pater pauperum,
veni, dator munerum,
veni, lumen cordium.
Consolator optime,
dulcis hospes animae,
dulce refrigerium.
In labore requies,
in aestu temperies,
in fletu solacium.
O lux beatissima,
reple cordis intima
tuorum fidelium.
Sine tuo numine,
nihil est in homine,
nihil est innoxium.
Lava quod est sordidum,
riga quod est aridum,
sana quod est saucium.
Flecte quod est rigidum,
fove quod est frigidum,
rege quod est devium.
Da tuis fidelibus,
in te confidentibus,
sacrum septenarium.
Da virtutis meritum,
da salutis exitum,
da perenne gaudium.

Dominica Pentecostes; Sequentia

Vocabulary: *pauperum* / *munerum* / *cordium*: of the poor / of gifts / of hearts
optime (vocative): excellent
in labore / *in aestu* / *in fletu*: during toil / heat / tears
beatissimus -a -um: most blessed
tuorum fidelium: of your faithful
sine tuo numine: without your power
tuis fidelibus confidentibus: to your faithful people believing
septenarius -a -um: seven-fold

1. First, translate all the verb forms in italics. Give the alternative "B type," or future / legal form, for that verb. Then reverse both forms.

2. Explain the ending you see in the words *dulcis*; *dulce*; *perenne*. Give the noun with which each word agrees.

3. What is the omitted antecedent for all of those *quods*?

4. Looking ahead, given how the word appears in the dictionary, what function do you see in the words *lucis*, *cordis*, *virtutis*, and *salutis*?

Biblia Vulgata, Hieronymus (347–420 PC)

Dicit ei Iesus: "Iam noli me tangere, nondum enim ascendi ad Patrem; vade autem ad fratres meos. . . ."

Evangelium Secundum Ioannem 20.17

Vocabulary: *ei*: to her

1. How else could the phrase *noli me tangere* be expressed in Latin?

Tu statuisti omnes terminos terrae,
aestatem et hiemem, tu plasmasti ea.
Memor esto huius:
inimicus improperavit Domino,
et populus insipiens sprevit nomen tuum.

Psalmus 74 (73).17–18

Vocabulary: *plasmare*: to form, fashion
huius: of this thing
improperare: to taunt
insipiens, insipientis: foolish, unwise

1. If *terrae* is not subject plural then which function is it? (We will properly, officially address this function really soon . . .)

---

2. Give the reverse form of *omnes terminus* and *ea*.

---

3. Using the "B" (future / comic / legal) imperative, say in Latin: "They shall be mindful!"

---

4. Reverse the last line.

LUDUS 5

AFTER LESSONS 13–15

Topics covered: *Block 2 nouns and adjectives; A and B imperatives.*

A.

REGINALDUS FOSTER (1939–2020 PC)

OmnE claudE conclavE, specularIA reserA cunctA. TotAM eiciAM pigritiAM.

Ludorum Domesticorum Ridicula

Vocabulary: *specularia -orum* (n pl): windows

1. Translate the brain-teaser!

____

____

Among his youthful pastoral poems, *Eclogae*, Rome's greatest poet, Publius Vergilius Maro (70–19 AC), has left a mystical, sublime piece about a Golden Age and the arrival of a savior.

B.

Utima Cumaei venit iam carminis aetas;
. . .
iam redit et Virgo, redeunt Saturnia regna,
iam nova progenies caelo demittitur alto.
. . .
ferrea primum
desinet ac toto surget gens aurea mundo,
casta fave Lucina: tuus iam regnat Apollo.
. . .
ille deum vitam accipiet . . .
pacatumque reget patriis virtutibus orbem.

Eclogae 4.4–17

Vocabulary:
Cumaei . . . carminis: of the Cumaean-Sibyl's song (about the ages of the world)
Virgo: the goddess of Justice
Saturnius -a -um: belonging to Saturn (primitive, first, unspoiled)
demittitur: he/she/it is sent down
caelo . . . alto: from heaven on high
toto . . . mundo: over the whole world
Lucina: Diana, sister of Apollo, goddess of childbirth (among other things)
ille: he (the newborn child)
deum = *deorum*: of the gods
patriis virtutibus: with his father's virtues

1. State which adjectives agree with the following nouns:

a. *aetas* ____________________
b. *gens* (2) ____________________
c. *Apollo* ____________________
d. *orbem* ____________________
e. *Lucina* ____________________

2. The verbs in the text are: *venire* (to come), *redire* (to return), *desinere* (to cease), *surgere* (to rise up), *regnare* (to reign), *accipere* (to receive), *regere* (to rule). State the time of each verb and translate it (*redeunt* = *rediunt*).

3. From the verb *paco, pacare, pacavi, pacatum* (to placate, pacify), what does the form *pacatus -a -um* mean alone here?

4. From the verb *faveo, favere, favi, fautum* (to favor, indulge, look favorably), what from do you see in "*fave*" in the text? Give the reverse form of "*fave.*" What other way have you learnt of expressing that form in Latin?

5. Write out your translation of the verses of Vergil.

6. If the infinitive of the verb is *accipere*, why did Vergil write *accipiet* for that time? Explain fully. Give the other five times of that same verb, keeping the subject the same.

C.

ipsae lacte domum referent distenta capellae
ubera, nec magnos metuent armenta leones;
ipsa tibi blandos fundent cunabula flores.
occidet et serpens, et fallax herba veneni

Eclogae 4.21–24

Vocabulary: *ipsae / ipsa*: themselves
domum = ad domum
lacte: with milk
armentum -i (n): head of cattle
tibi: for you

1. What is the dictionary problem with nouns and adjectives from Block 2? Find the dictionary entry for the following words:

   a. *leones* ________________________

   b. *flores* ________________________

   c. *ubera* ________________________

   d. *serpens* ________________________

2. What totally different functions are possible for both *leones* and *flores*?

____

3. Check your dictionary and give the different meanings of the totally distinct verbs *occīdo* and *occĭdo*. Which verb is being used in this text?

____

____

4. If all the verbs in the text are Group 3, what time is Vergil using throughout the text?

____

5. Give the *ego* form for those same verbs, keeping the time the same. Now give the T.1 forms for those same verbs, keeping the same subject as you see in the text.

6. Translate Vergil's lines.

7. What do these variations mean exactly:

   a. *magnus metuebam armentum Leo*

   b. *occīdet et serpentem et fallacem herbam veneni*

   c. *ipsas lacte domum referimus distentas capellas*

8. Write in Latin: "Pour out warm [*calidus, fervidus*] milk for [preposition] our nourishment, just as [*sicut, ut, velut*] you poured out multicolored [*varius -a -um*] flowers for our delight [*oblectatio -onis* (f)]." Put the verbs at the end of their phrases.

9. Now reverse every word in your Latin sentence.

D.

“Talia saecla” suis dixerunt “currite” fusis
. . .
Parcae.
. . . Incipe, parve puer, risu cognoscere matrem
(matri longa decem tulerunt fastidia menses)
incipe, parve puer.

Eclogae 4.46–62

Vocabulary: *suis . . . fusis*: to their spindles (weaving history)
Parcae: the three fates
parve puer: O little boy!
risu: with a smile
matri: to your mother
fastidium -i (n): nausea, annoyance

1. What forms do you see in *currite* and *incipe*? Reverse those forms, and give the alternative Latin formula for that use.

2. Translate the lines.

E.

macti virtute vos Clarenses estote

Dr. Charles Weiss, Clare College
Cambridge 2016

Vocabulary: *mactus -a -um*: honored, glorified
virtute: with valor, excellence
Clarensis -e: belonging to Clare College

1. Translate this good luck message!

2. Reverse *estote* and give the alternative Latin formula for that use.

LESSON 16

THE OF-POSSESSION FUNCTION (GENITIVE) FOR BLOCK 1 AND BLOCK 2 NOUNS AND ADJECTIVES

Two Uses of the Of-Possession Function (Genitive)

The genitive has two distinct uses:

1. to denote possession (e.g.: *the books of my father* or *my father's books*), or to whom an action refers (e.g.: *the arrival of Caesar* [subjective]);
2. to denote a relationship or feeling toward something (e.g., *hatred of unfairness, study of Latin, love of truth, cause of suffering* [objective]).

Both uses may safely be translated using the word "of."

As you have begun to learn, genitive singular endings are given by the dictionary as the second part of the noun. They will not be tabulated separately! **Genitive singular endings are found in the dictionary.** These endings are used for both nouns and adjectives.

Genitive Singular Endings

Block 1			*Block 2*		
lupus -**i**	(m),	a wolf	homo, **hominis**	(m),	a man
capella -**ae**	(f),	a she-goat	lex, **legis**	(f),	a law
aratrum -**i**	(n),	a plough	corpus, **corporis**	(n),	a body

Genitive Plural Endings

Block 1			*Block 2*
M	*F*	*N*	*M/F/N*
-orum	**-arum**	**-orum**	**-um / -ium** 80/20 nouns 20/80 adjectives

Traps

You have a third calculation to bear in mind when analyzing words from Block 1 and Block 2. Many of the of-possession endings are identical to other endings, especially subject endings (especially for masculine & feminine Block 1 nouns and adjectives). This can lead to confusion and ambiguity. Does *amici mei habent pecuniam* mean "my friends have money"? Or "they have the money of my friend"? Not even the angels....

Up to now, the ending *-um* has been predominantly a singular object ending, or neuter subject ending. For a Block 2 word, the *-um* ending is genitive plural.

Combining nouns and adjectives from Block 1 and Block 2 gets even more dicey, so always check how the word you are reading appears in the dictionary:

bonum patrum officium omnium nos tenet

The good duty of all fathers holds us.

As a matter of style the Romans loved to put the of-possession words out in front:

veritatis splendor

the splendor of truth

per sanctorum tuorum preces

through the prayers of your saints

Classical Latin Translation Practice

Albius Tibullus (c. 55–19 AC)

Me retinent vinctum formosae vincla puellae,
Et sedeo duras ianitor ante fores.

Elegiae 1.1.55

Vocabulary: *vinclum -i* (n): fetter, chain

1. From the verb *vincio, vincire*, what must *vinctum* mean? Who is *vinctum* in this line?

2. Write in Latin: "The hard doors of the beautiful girls will shut me out [*excludere*]."

O fuge te tenerae puerorum credere turbae,
Nam causam iusti semper amoris habent.

Elegiae 1.4.9

Vocabulary: *fugio, fugere*: avoid
tenerae turbae: to the tender crowd
credere: to entrust

1. What other less common translation of PP2 was given as a footnote to Lesson 8? This will work well here.

2. What special group of verbs does *fugio* belong to? Think carefully before giving the reverse form of *fuge*.

3. What is ambiguous about the word *iusti* in the second half of this sentence? Provide two alternative translations for the second line, then indicate which one will make more sense here.

Titus Lucretius Carus (c. 99–c. 55 AC)

Aeneadum genetrix, hominum divomque voluptas,
alma Venus, caeli subter labentia signa
quae mare navigerum, quae terras frugiferentis
concelebras, per te quoniam genus omne animantum
concipitur visitque exortum lumina solis:
te, dea, te fugiunt venti, te nubila caeli
adventumque tuum, tibi suavis daedala tellus
summittit flores, tibi rident aequora ponti
placatumque nitet diffuso lumine caelum.

De Rerum Natura 1.1–9

Vocabulary: *Aeneades, Aeneadum* (m pl): the descendants of Aeneas
divom = deorum
labens, labentis: gliding, slipping
quoniam: because
animans, animantis: living thing
concipitur: he/she/it is conceived
exortus -a -um: having come into being
nubilum -i (n): cloud, cloudy sky
tibi: for you
daedalus -a -um: skillful, creative
diffuso lumine: with light having been spread about

1. Identify the time and translate: *concelebras, visit, fugiunt, summittit, rident, nitet*. Now give the T.3 forms for those same verbs, keeping the subject the same.

2. Which verb must link with both *quae* clauses? Who is the antecedent of that *quae*?

3. Which verbs link with *quoniam* (one of these verbs is given in the vocabulary)?

4. Look back at the notes to Lesson 13 and explain how *frugiferentis* can be describing *terras*, and how *suavis* can be describing *flores*.

5. From the verb *placare*, "to calm, pacify," what does *placatus -a -um* mean?

6. Find all the genitives in the text (there are eight).

7. Have a go at translating this sublime invocation of Venus that opens Lucretius's great epic poem about the nature of things.

Post-Classical Latin Translation Practice

Thomas Aquinas (1225–1274 PC)

Here are some sentences from Thomas's *Quaestiones Quodlibetales*, which he gleaned from debates among his students in Paris and Naples.

1. What is the meaning of *qui-libet, quae-libet, quod-libet* in the dictionary?

2. The adjective created from that word is *quodlibetalis -e*. To which block does this adjective belong? What gender and function do you see in *quodlibetales*? Give the reverse form of both words in the title to his work.

Dicitur (1 Cor 11.14): "Animalis homo non percipit ea quae Dei sunt; spiritualis autem iudicat omnia," et praecipue quantum ad ea quae sunt fidei, quia fides est donum Dei et ideo interpretatio sermonum numeratur inter alia dona Spiritus Sancti.

Quodlibet 12 Quaestio 17

Vocabulary: *dicitur / numeratur* (T.1 passive): it is said / it is numbered
praecipue: especially
quantum: what pertains
fidei: of the faith
Spiritus: of the Spirit

1. If the word is *deus, dei* (m), then *dei* can function as what two things in a Latin sentence? What is the more likely translation for *ea quae sunt Dei*?

2. What is the difficulty in analyzing the words *donum* and *sermonum*? Give the reverse form of each word.

3. What is the reverse form of *omnia*?

[Objection:] Praeterea, labor manualis necessarius est ad sustentationem vitae corporalis, sicut actus virtutum sunt necessarii ad sustentationem vitae spiritualis. Sed actus virtutum sunt in praecepto. Ergo et laborare manibus.

Quodlibet 7 Quaestio 7

Vocabulary: *actus* (subject pl): actions
in praecepto: in the law
manibus: with the hands

[Counter Objection:] Usus liberalium artium nobilior est quam mechanicarum quia in opere manuali constitit. Sed usus liberalium artium non est in praecepto. Ergo multo minus labor manuum.

Quodlibet 7 Quaestio 7

Vocabulary: *usus* (subject sing): the use
nobilior (subject): more noble
quam: than
in opere manuali: in manual work
multo minus: much less
manuum: of the hands

1. What two ways were given in Lesson 8 (table footnote) for translating PP2? Give two translations for *laborare*.

2. What five different functions are possible for the adjectives in the text *manualis*, *corporalis*, *spiritualis*? Why is it so necessary to apply that knowledge to this sentence?

3. According to the rules for Block 2 nouns and adjectives, what percentage ending, 80% or 20%, applies to the adjective *liberalium* in the text? And what percentage to the noun *artium*?

4. After translating the text, explain what would be ambiguous about *Ad sustentationem vitae terristris labor necessarius est.*

Reginaldus Foster (1939–2020)

VestrorUM egregiUM nobiliUM ducUM beneficiUM eximiUM laudUM singulariUM praeconiUM habebit.

Ludorum Domesticorum Ridicula

Vocabulary: *praeconium -i* (n): celebrating, commendation

1. Find and translate the verb. Then label all the other words as Block 1 or Block 2 before attempting to translate the whole!

LESSON 17

THE PASSIVE VOICE IN TIMES 4-5-6

Meaning of the Passive Times in English

So far we have met verbs in the six times in the indicative **active voice** (*ago, agere, egi, actus* …). These verbs can be manipulated to appear in the same six times but in the **passive voice**, that is, when the subject of the verb is suffering (*patior, pati, passus sum* …) the action of the verb rather than acting upon it. The person *by whom* the action of a passive verb is being done is called the **agent**.

This is how the six times sound in the passive voice in English:

Time	*One Latin Example*	*English Meanings*
Time 1 *present tense*	**amantur**	they are loved they are being loved
Time 2 *imperfect tense* continuous, repeated, or frustrated action in the past; a moving film	**cantabatur**	it was being sung it used to be sung it was always sung it would be sung
Time 3 *future tense*	**audieris**	you will be heard you will be being heard
Time 4: one form, two distinct times		
Time 4a *present perfect tense*	**dicta sum**	I have been said
Time 4b *past simple/perfect tense* snapshot in the past	**dicta sum**	I was said (*take care to differentiate from T.2*)
Time 5 *pluperfect tense*	**visi eramus**	we had been seen
Time 6 *future perfect tense*	**scriptae eritis**	you will have been written

The True Passive Has No Object

Just as with the verb "to be," **with a true passive verb there is no direct object**.

> Henry was crowned king. I am spoken of as their friend. I was made unhappy.

Henry and king, I and friend, I and unhappy, all are in the subject function (nominative case).

How to Form the Passive in Times 4-5-6

Times 4-5-6 passive are made up of two components, a two-word formula:

Component 1	*Component 2*
PP4 (made to agree with the subject of the verb) singular options: *laudatus -a -um* plural options: *laudati -ae -a*	**Time 1, 2 or 3 of the verb "to be" (*esse*)** Ending on *esse* shows the subject: singular: *o/m – s – t* plural: *mus – tis – nt*

Times 4-5-6 Passive

Time 4 passive	PP4 *laudatus -a -um* + T.1 of *esse*: *sum, es, est,* *sumus, estis, sunt*	***est*** *puella dives* ***facta*** The girl **has been** or **was made** rich.
Time 5 passive	PP4 *laudatus -a -um* + T.2 of *esse* *eram, eras, erat,* *eramus, eratis, erant*	*dives* ***factus erat*** *vir* The man **had been made** rich.
Time 6 passive	PP4 *laudatus -a -um* + T.3 of *esse* *ero, eris, erit* *erimus, eritis, erunt*	***facti*** *divites* ***erunt*** *homines* The men **will have been made** rich.

Placing the Parts

This formula can be misleading, since, on their own, these two components retain the meanings already learned (e.g., *laudatus* = having been praised, and *sum* = I am), but in combination they produce the completely different passive voice meanings of T.4-5-6 (e.g., *laudatus sum* = I have been praised, I was praised). Worse still, the PP4 and the part of *esse* can be separated in a sentence by many other words, and the part of *esse* will often precede the PP4, since Romans did not like finishing a sentence with words of one syllable. This makes the passive T.4-5-6 formula difficult to spot.

sum copiose laudatus

I was abundantly praised.

As usual, read the whole Latin sentence before you start, as you never know what is going to happen before you get to the end.

Examples

Flavia est optima discipula inter nos heri iudicata.

Flavia was judged the best scholar among us yesterday.

When you start reading, the temptation is to assume the sentence begins, "Flavia is the best scholar...," but when you get to *iudicata*, you realise that it must be T.4 passive of *iudico, iudicare*, "Flavia was judged..."

Voces assidue prope urbem auditae erant.

Voices had been heard continually near the city.

In each example, note how the adjective part of the passive construction (PP4) has to agree with the subject of the passive verb: in the example above, *voces* is feminine plural, hence *auditae*.

Classical Latin Translation Practice

Gaius Julius Caesar (100–44 AC)

Multum erat frumentum provisum et convectum superioribus temporibus, multum ex omni provincia comportabatur; magna copia pabuli suppetebat.

Bellum Civile 49

Vocabulary: *providere*: to provide for
superibus temporibus: at earlier times
ex omni provincia: from the whole province
comportabatur: [T.2 passive]
copia -ae (f): abundance, resource

1. Say in Latin: "Many resources were provided for and will have been gathered together."

Gaius Suetonius Tranquillus (c. 69–c. 122 PC)

Solusque omnium ex iis, qui pari lege damnati erant, restitutus in patriam amplissimos honores percucurrit. (*De Vitis Caesarum, Vita Neronis* 3.2)

Vocabulary: *ex iis*: from among those people
pari lege: by the same law
amplissimus -a -um: greatest, most distinguished

1. What function do you see in the ending of *omnium*?

2. Identify the passive verb time of *damnati erant*. Say in Latin: "He will have been condemned" and "They-women were condemned."

3. From the verb *restituo* (I restore), what does a plain-simple PP4 *restitutus* mean?

4. Reverse the phrase *restitutus in patriam amplissimos honores percucurrit*.

Et subinde matre etiam relegata paene inops atque egens apud amitam Lepidam nutritus est. (*De Vitis Caesarum, Vita Neronis* 6.3)

Vocabulary: *matre relegata*: because his mother had been banished
egens, egentis: needy, very poor

1. From the verb *nutrio* (I rear, bring up), explain the verb time and voice you see in *nutritus est*. How can we tell the gender of the subject from that form?

2. Look back at the list of prepositions in Lesson 6, and pick a suitable meaning for *apud* here.

3. Say in Latin: "We mothers, helpless and needy, had been brought up at the houses of our aunts."

Verum . . . non solum paternas opes reciperavit, sed et Crispi Passieni vitrici sui hereditate ditatus est. (*De Vitis Caesarum, Vita Neronis* 6.3)

Vocabulary: *verum* [here, and frequently] but
suus -a -um: his
hereditate: by an inheritance

1. Hunt around in the dictionary to find the Block 2 crazy subject form for *opes*. The adjective *paternas*, together with the ending on the verb, gives you the clue that the phrase must be performing what function here?

---

2. Give two possible translations for the passive verb time *ditatus est*.

---

3. What function do you see in the words *vitrici sui*?

---

4. Say in Latin: "They will have been enriched by an inheritance of their stepfathers."

---

deinceps eiusdem saepe lectica per publicum simul vectus est. (*De Vitis Caesarum, Vita Neronis* 9.1)

Vocabulary: *eiusdem . . . lectica*: in the litter of that same woman

---

Post-Classical Latin Translation Practice

PETRUS VENERABILIS (1092–1156 AC)

sic rerum ordo mutatus est, sic pax ecclesiastica inter plurimos perturbata est, ut corporis Christi membra contra se invicem insurgant.

Epistularum Liber Unus, Epistola 2 (to Matthew, Bishop of Albano)

Vocabulary: *rerum*: of things
plurimus -a -um: most, very many
ut: that
insurgant: they rise up

1. What passive verb time do you identify in the forms *mutatus est* and *perturbata est*? Why did the author correctly end one PP4 in *-us* and the other in *-a*?

2. What plural subject form must be the subject of *insurgant*?

3. What new function do you recognize in the endings of *corporis* and *Christi*? There are different reasons for this function, but which word is always a safe translation?

Serenam diem tenebrosa nubila contexerunt, nitentes solis radios caliginosi aeris fumositas obduxit, meridianus fulgor taeterrimarum repente umbrarum faciem induit. Rerum natura mutata est, oriens in occasum conversus est, ignis praevalidus subito exstinctus est, funis argenteus ruptus est, amicus ab amico disiunctus est.

Epistularum Liber Unus, Epistola 5 (to Ato, Bishop of Troyes)

Vocabulary: *nitens, nitentis*: shining
fumositas, fumositatis (f): smokiness
aer, aeris (m): air
taeterrimus -a -um: most hideous
faciem (object): appearance
oriens, orientis (m): the east
occasum (object): the west
ab amico: from friend

1. The following pairs of adjectives and nouns agree: *serenam diem, nitentes radios, caliginosi aeris, meridianus fulgor, ignis praevalidus, funis argenteus*. Explain fully how the endings on the words in each pair can look so different, and yet match in terms of function, number, and gender.

2. What verb time and voice do you see in these constructions: *mutata est, conversus est, exstinctus est, ruptus est, disiunctus est*? Identify the subject of each verb and translate each phrase in two possible ways. Reverse each verbal form.

3. Say in Latin: "Our friendship [*amicitia*] had been changed, and the very strong fires of my love [*amor*] had been extinguished."

Episcoporum atque abbatum plurimi ad proxima castra violenter abducti sunt, et quidam eorum post verbera et vulnera barbarica immanitate incarcerati sunt.

Epistularum Liber Unus, Epistola 27
(to Pope Innocent)

Vocabulary: *abbas, abbatis* (m): abbot
proximus -a -um: nearest
violenter: violently
qui-dam, quae-dam, quod-dam: a certain
eorum: of them
barbarica immanitate: with barbarous cruelty

1. Give the reverse form of *verbera* and *vulnera*. What does the subject singular form remind us about Block 2 nouns?

2. From the verbs *abducere* (to lead away) and *incarcerare* (to imprison), what time and voice do you read in the text?

3. What new function ending do you see in *Episcoporum* and *Abbatum*? What is potentially confusing about the ending on *Abbat-um*?

LESSON 18

WAYS OF ASKING QUESTIONS

Particles

There are three particles one can put into an ordinary statement that will turn it into a question. Each particle gives the question a different emphasis.

ne?

is placed on the end of a word (as a suffix). It turns a statement into a question and puts the emphasis of the question on the word it is attached to.

puerumne amas? — *Do you love the boy?*

nonne?

included in a statement turns it into a question that expects the answer "yes."

nonne puerum amas? — *Surely you love the boy?*
You love the boy, don't you?

num?

included in a statement turns it into a question that expects the answer "no."

num puerum amas? — *Surely you don't love the boy?*
You don't love the boy, do you?

Question Words

Here are a handful of question words (of course there are many more …)

cur? quare? quamobrem?	*why?*
quando?	*when?*
quo?	*to where? whither?*
quousque?	*how far? how long?*
unde?	*from where?*
quomodo? ut?	*in what way? how?*
quot?	*how many?*
ubi?	*where? or when?*
quam? [+ basic adjective]	*how?*
qualis, quale?	*what sort of?*
quantus, quanta, quantum?	*how big? how much?*
qui?	*how? why?*
quid?	*how? why?*

Interrogative Pronoun

quis (m/f), quid (n)?	*who, what, what sort of?*

The interrogative pronoun shares the endings of the relative pronoun for the other functions and numbers.

qui, quae, quod?	*who, what, what sort of?*

Classical Latin Translation Practice

Gaius Valerius Catullus (84–54 AC)

scelesta, vae te! quae tibi manet vita?
quis nunc te adibit? cui videberis bella?
quem nunc amabis? . . .
quem basiabis?

Carmina 8

Vocabulary: *vae te!*: woe to you!
tibi: to you
adire: to approach
cui videberis: to whom will you seem . . .

1. From the verb *maneo, manere*, what verb time do you see in *manet*? Give the other five verb times keeping the subject the same.

2. From their endings, you will quickly recognize the verb time of *adibit*, *amabis*, and *basiabis*. Give the *I* form and the *they* form for that verb time.

3. What is the meaning of *quae* as a question word?

4. What function do you see in the form *quem*?

eone nomine, urbis o piissimi,
socer generque, perdidistis omnia?

Carmina 29

Vocabulary: *eo nomine*: on this account
piissimus -a -um: most honorable
perdere: to destroy, ruin

1. Fully explain the use of *ne* as a suffix.

---

2. Refer to Lesson 5 and explain what you have to do when you come across an adjective on its own in a Latin sentence. This should help you deal properly with *piissimi* and *omnia*.

---

3. From the word *urbs, urbis* (f): city, what is the meaning of *urbis*? Give the reverse form (20%).

---

num facta impia fallacum hominum caelicolis placent?

Carmina 30

Vocabulary: *factum -i* (n): a deed
fallax, fallacis: deceitful
caelicolis: to the gods
placere: to be pleasing

1. What function do you see in the words *fallacum hominum*?

2. What kind of answer does a question starting with *num* expect?

3. Say in Latin: "Surely the wicked deed of a deceitful man will not be pleasing to you [*tibi*]?"

nullane res potuit crudelis flectere mentis consilium?

Carmina 64

Vocabulary: *res* (f subject): thing, circumstance

1. From the verb *possum, posse, potui* (to be able), identify the time of *potuit*. Give the other five verb times, keeping the subject the same.

2. What form of the verb would you expect to follow the verb *posse*?

3. What is ambiguous about *crudelis*? What is ambiguous about *consilium*?

4. Explain how detailed analysis of the sentence can help resolve these ambiguities.

Post-Classical Latin Translation Practice

QUINTUS SEPTIMUS FLORENS TERTULLIANUS (C. 155–C. 240 PC)

Quis hoc sustinere aut defendere potest?

De Idololatria 14

Vocabulary: *hoc* (object): this thing

1. What does *quis* mean as a question word? Here it is functioning as the subject of which verb?

2. Give the other five times of *potest*, keeping the subject the same.

sed iam hic responde, interfector veritatis: nonne vere crucifixus est deus? . . . nonne vere resuscitatus est ut vere scilicet mortuus?

De Carne Christi 5

Vocabulary: *hic*: at this point
vere: truly
ut: as
mortuus -a -um: dead

1. What special mood of the verb do you spot in *responde*? Taking care to put the verb in the right group, give the reverse form.

2. From the verbs *cruci-figere* (to crucify) and *resuscitare* (raise up, resurrect), what time and voice do you identify in the text?

---

3. What sort of answer is expected by a question starting with the word *nonne*?

---

4. Say in Latin: "The truth had been destroyed [*delere*] and will not have been resurrected again."

Haec erunt corpora nostra quae Romanos obsecrat exhibere hostiam vivam sanctam placabilem deo. quomodo "vivam" si peritura sunt? quomodo "sanctam" si profana sunt? quomodo "placabilem" si damnata sunt?

De Resurrectione Carnis 47

Vocabulary: *haec* (n pl): these
exhibere: to present as
deo: to God
periturus -a -um: destined to die
profanus -a -um: unholy, profane
damnare: to condemn, doom

1. Reading through the first sentence, you come across the relative pronoun *quae*. Look back at Lessons 10 and 11, and explain how you are going to approach translating the sentence (word order, antecedent, etc.).

---

2. Identify the verb times in *erunt*, *sunt*, and *damnata sunt*.

3. Given that it looks so different, how can *placabilem* be describing *hostiam* as well as *vivam* and *sanctam*?

4. Leave out *haec*, and leaving *deo* the same, reverse the first sentence.

unde malum et quare? et unde homo et quomodo?

De Praescriptione Haereticorum 7

1. Reverse *malum* and *homo*.

LUDUS 6

AFTER LESSONS 16–18

Topics covered: *genitive of nouns and adjectives; meaning of the six times in the passive voice; T.4-5-6 passive; ways of asking questions.*

A.

1. In the reading for Lesson 16, how did Lucretius say (selected words): "Nurturing Venus, you visit the ship-bearing sea, the fruit-bearing lands under the slipping constellations of the sky"?

2. Write in Latin: "Through [preposition] Venus [check dictionary!] and Venus's love toward [preposition] us, the lands had been visited, around [preposition] which the ship-bearing seas [*mare* = 20%] were located [*collocare*]."

One of Rome's four great elegiac poets, Albius Tibullus (60–19 AC), has a few smooth and sweet lines of perfect Latin for your enjoyment and progress. First, like Vergil in his *Eclogue*, talking about a golden age.

B.

Quam bene Saturno vivebant rege, priusquam
Tellus in longas est patefacta vias!

Elegiae 1.3.35–36

Vocabulary: *quam bene*: how well!
Saturno … rege: when Saturn was king
priusquam: before
tellus, telluris (f): the land, earth

1. What meaning do you give to *est* on its own?

2. From the verb *patefacio, patefacere, patefeci, patefactum* (open up, expand), what does the form *patefactus -a -um* mean on its own?

3. State what voice / time the combination formula of *est* + *patefacta* produces, with what possible English translations?

4. What gender is *patefacta* and why?

5. Translate the lines.

6. Reverse line 36.

C.

He addresses a naked statue of Priapus.

Quae <u>tua</u> formosos cepit <u>sollertia</u>? <u>certe</u>
Non <u>tibi</u> barba nitet, non <u>tibi</u> culta <u>coma</u> est,
Nudus et hibernae <u>producis</u> frigora brumae,
Nudus et aestivi tempora sicca <u>Canis</u>.

Elegiae 1.4.3–6

Vocabulary: *tuus -a -um*: your, of yours
sollertia -ae (f): skill, shrewdness
certe: certainly, for sure
tibi: for you
coma -ae (f): hair
producere: to draw out, pass
canis -is (m): the dog star (which rises in late July)

1. When you see an adjective on its own in a Latin sentence, what must you do? Explain fully with reference to *formosos*.

2. Where do you find *frigora* and *tempora* in the dictionary?

3. If the verb is *colo, colere, colui, cultum* (take care of, adorn), then what time of that verb is being used in the text? Why the ending on *culta*?

4. What tempting translation is totally outlawed for *est culta*?

5. What two functions can nouns like *canis* have? What is the solution to choosing the correct option in this text?

6. What does *canis* mean as a verb (*cano, canere* ...)?

7. With what word or idea does *nudus* agree?

8. Translate the Latin.

9. In the dictionary, find the meaning of the following words:

a. *comis -e*

b. *comes, comitis*

c. *como, comere*

d. *coma -ae* (f)

10. What is the meaning of this Latin phrase: *quando comis comes comes comas*?

11. Omit the *tibi* for now and reverse lines 4–6.

D.

The opening verses of his wonderful poem about peace, where he condemns the inventor of weapons.

Quis fuit, horrendos primus qui protulit enses?
Quam ferus et vere ferreus ille fuit!
Tum caedes hominum generi, tum proelia nata,
Tum brevior dirae mortis aperta via est.

Elegiae 1.10.1–4

Vocabulary: *horrendus -a -um*: [cf. dictionary under *horreo*]
proferre: to bring forth
ensis -is (m): sword
quam: how!
vere: truly
ille, illa, illud = is, ea, id
generi: to-for the race
nascor, nasci, natus: to be born
dirus -a -um: dire, terrible

1. Point out the of-possession genitive forms in the text. Reverse each one.

2. If the verb is *aperio, aperire,* what voice and time do you see in the text, with which English meanings?

3. If the word is *brevior* (m & f), *brevius* (n), *brevioris,* meaning "shorter," which noun is it describing in the text? With which noun does *horrendos* agree?

4. Translate the lines, paying particular attention to *caedes nata* [*est*] and *proelia nata* [*sunt*].

5. Write in Latin, starting with the relative box: "The producers [*effector -oris* (m)] of horrendous swords [*ensus*—20%] will have been called [*voco, vocare*] savage and iron-like, through whom atrocious [*atrox, atrocis*] ways of dire deaths [*mors*—20%] had been opened."

E.

At nobis, Pax alma, veni spicamque teneto,
Perfluat et pomis candidus ante sinus.

Elegiae 1.10.67–8

Vocabulary:
nobis: for us
spica -ae (f): tuft, spike, ear of grain
teneo, tenere: hold
perfluat: may overflow, abound
pomis: with apples, fruits
ante (adv.): in front
sinus: lap, fold of cloth = apron

1. Look up the verb *venio, venire* in the dictionary and use the quantity markings there to figure out the difference in meaning between *vēni* and *venī*. They are completely different forms of the verb!

2. Give the reverse of each form, *vēni* and *venī*.

3. What part of speech is *teneto*? What does it mean?

4. Translate the Latin.

LESSON 19

THE OF-POSSESSION FUNCTION (GENITIVE) FOR RELATIVE PRONOUNS

In Latin, the relative pronouns are

Qui, quae, quod *who, which*

In English, the genitive function of the relative pronoun is expressed as follows:

of whom
of which
whose

Only these three translations are possible, regardless of the gender and number of the antecedent being referred to.

The relative pronoun *relates* to something outside of its own phrase (the relative clause or box). This something is called the **antecedent**. The relative pronoun derives its gender and number from the antecedent. It derives its function from the job it is doing in its own relative box.

Antecedent is...	*Relative pronoun is* **genitive** *in relative box*
masculine, feminine, and neuter singular	**cuius**
masculine or neuter plural	**quorum**
feminine plural	**quarum**

librum cuius nescio auctorem legi.

I read a book whose author I do not know.

I read a book the author of which I do not know.

Triginta mihi quattuorque messes
Tecum, si memini, fuere, Iuli.
Quarum dulcia mixta sunt amaris,
Sed iucunda tamen fuere plura.

M. Valerius Martialis, *Epigrammata* 12.34

To me there were thirty-four harvests
with you, Julius, if I remember,
Of which the sweet things were mingled with bitter things,
But even so there were more agreeable things.

- Identify the relative pronoun. What verb must go with it? What is the antecedent of the relative pronoun?

- What is the verb *fuere* a short form of?

Classical Latin Translation Practice

Lucius Apuleius Madaurensis (c. 124–c. 170 AC)

Frustra me pastor ille cuius iustitiam fidemque magnus comprobavit Iuppiter ob eximiam speciem tantis praetulit deabus.

Metamorphoses 4.30

Vocabulary: *ille* (subject): that
praefero, praeferre: to prefer
tantis deabus: to such great goddesses

1. Identify the relative pronoun and identify which verb belongs in the relative box. Who is the subject of that verb?

2. Which verb must be the main verb? Who is the subject of that verb? Who is the object of that verb?

3. Note down the three possible translations of *cuius*. Identify the antecedent of *cuius* and select the translation which works best for *cuius*.

Itur ad constitutum scopulum montis ardui, cuius in summo cacumine statutam puellam cuncti deserunt.

Metamorphoses 4.35

Vocabulary: *itur*: it is gone, or she goes
in summo cacumine: on the highest peak

1. From the verb *constituere* (to appoint, arrange), what is the meaning of *constitutum*? From the verb *statuere* (to place, establish), what is the meaning of *statutum*?

2. Which verb belongs with *cuius*? Give the subject and then the object of that verb.

3. Write in Latin: "All women will desert the appointed rocks of the lofty mountains [*mons*—20%]."

Nos, quarum voces accipis, tuae famulae sedulo tibi praeministrabimus.

Metamorphoses 5.2

Vocabulary: *accipere*: (here) to hear
tibi: to you
praeministrare: attend, administer

1. Look up the adjective *sedulus -a -um* in the dictionary. You should find under that entry the meaning of the adverb *sedulo*.

2. Given the form of the relative pronoun, what gender is *nos*?

Nec sunt enim beati quorum divitias nemo novit.

Metamorphoses 5.10.26

Vocabulary: *nosco, noscere, novi, notus*: come to know about

1. When you meet an adjective like *beati*, on its own in a sentence, what must you do?

2. Identify the verb in the relative clause, its subject, and its object.

Post-Classical Latin Translation Practice

Gregorius I (540–604 PC)

Praestet hoc nobis Deitas beata
Patris ac Nati, pariterque Sancti
Spiritus, cuius resonat per omnem gloria mundum.

"Ecce iam noctis"

Vocabulary: *praestet hoc nobis*: may he/she/it discharge this for us
pariter: also, likewise
spiritus: of the spirit

1. Find the subject noun-adjective pair that is doing the verb *praestet*.

2. Identify the relative box here. Identify the subject and the verb within the box.

3. What three meanings can be assigned to *cuius*? Which one will sound best here?

Rabanus Maurus (776–856 PC)

Sit, Christe, tibi gloria
cum Patre et Sancto Spiritu,
quorum luce mirifica
sancti congaudent perpetim.

"Iesu salvator saeculi"

Vocabulary: *sit … tibi*: may there be to you
cum Patre et Sancto Spiritu: with the Father and the Holy Spirit
luce mirifica: by the wondrous light

1. Look up the adjective *perpes, perpetis*. You should find the meaning of the adverb *perpetim* listed there.

2. Identify the antecedents of *quorum*.

3. In the *quorum* clause, identify the subject and verb.

4. Translate *quorum luce mirifica* in two different, but equally correct, ways, according to the only possible translations for that form of the relative pronoun.

Thomas Aquinas (1225–1274 PC)

me immundum munda tuo sanguine; cuius una stilla salvum facere totum mundum quit ab omni scelere.

"Adoro te devote"

Vocabulary: *tuo sanguine*: with your blood
quit: he/she/it is able
ab omni scelere: from every wrong

1. What does the position of *me immundum* in the line remind us about the perennial nature of Latin word order?

2. In what one area have we learned that Latin word order follows a fixed rule?

3. Given that rule, identify the main verb, and identify the verb that must belong with *cuius*.

4. If *munda* is a verb, then what mood is it? Give the reverse form.

5. What is the antecedent of *cuius*?

6. What is the subject of *quit*?

---

7. From the verb *facio, facere, feci, factus*, give the meaning of *facere.*

Liturgia Romana, Paulus VI (1897–1978 PC)

Hostias et preces tibi, Domine, laudis offerimus. Tu suscipe [eas] pro animabus illis, quarum hodie memoriam facimus.

Missa Pro Defunctis

Vocabulary: *tibi*: to you
pro animabus illis: on behalf of those souls

1. How do you disentangle the (apparent) problem of whether *laudis* comes from the verb *laudo* or the noun *laus*?

---

2. Reverse *laudis.*

---

3. Taking care to put the verb in the correct group, give the reverse form of *suscipe* and the "B" version for that same mood (Lesson 15).

---

4. Give two possible translations for the words *quarum memoriam facimus.*

LESSON 20

THE OF-POSSESSION FUNCTION (GENITIVE) FOR FIRST- AND SECOND-PERSON PRONOUNS

The genitive has two distinct uses:

1. to denote possession (e.g., *the books of my father* or *my father's books)*, or to whom an action refers (e.g., *the arrival of Caesar* [subjective]);
2. to denote a relationship or feeling toward something (e.g., *hatred of unfairness, study of Latin, love of truth, cause of suffering* [objective])

1. To denote possession, use the possessive adjective. These are all Block 1 adjectives.

meus -a -um	*my*
noster -tra -trum	*our*
tuus -a -um	*your*
vester -tra -trum	*your*
filiae meae sunt amantes.	*My daughters are loving.*

2. To denote a relationship or feeling toward me, us, or you, use the genitive of the pronoun.

mei	*of / toward me*
nostri	*of / toward us*
tui	*of / toward you*
vestri	*of / toward you*
filiae meae sunt amantes mei	*my daughters are loving towards me.*
amor nostri	*love for us*
memoria vestri	*the memory of you*

Where a number or part of the whole is indicated (partitive genitive), use *nostrum* and *vestrum*.

quis nostrum?	*who of us?*
nemo vestrum	*no one of you!*

curatio mei patris et curatio mei.
Taking care of my father and taking care of me.

pecunia mei patris et pecunia mea.
My father's money and my money.

accepisti pecuniam meam mei patrisque.
You received my money and the money of my father.

Classical Latin Translation Practice

Gaius Petronius Arbiter "Elegantiarum" (c. 27–66 PC)

Some episodes from the *Cena Trimalchionis* [Trimalchio's dinner]

plane etiam hoc servus tuus indicare potest; non enim aenigma est.

Satyricon 41

Vocabulary: *hoc* (object): this thing

1. Find the meaning of the adverb *plane* under the adjective *planus -a -um*.

2. Say in Latin: "We will be able to complete [*perficio*] our exercises [*exercitatio*], because they are not riddles!"

nemo nostrum solide natus est.

Satyricon 47

Vocabulary: *solide*: solidly
natus -a -um: born

1. Why did Petronius properly use the form *nostrum*, rather than *nostri*, in this excerpt?

laudatus Trimalchio hilarius bibit et iam ebrio proximus "nemo" inquit "vestrum rogat Fortunatam meam ut saltet? credite mihi: cordacem nemo melius ducit."

Satyricon 52

Vocabulary: *hilarius*: more cheerfully
ebrio: to (being) drunk [adjective]
proximus -a -um: very near
inquit: he/she/it said
ut saltet: to dance
mihi: (here) me
cordax, cordacis (m): the cordax, a lively Greek dance
melius: better

1. From the verb *laudo, laudare*, what does *laudatus* mean on its own? What would the clause *ubi laudatus erat* mean?

2. Why is *vestrum*, rather than *vestri*, the proper form to use in this context?

3. Identify the mood of the verb you see in *credite*. Give the reverse form.

4. Identify the time of the verbs *bibit, rogat*, and *ducit*. Give the T.3 form for each verb, keeping the subject the same.

ad dexteram mcam ponas statuam Fortunatae meae columbam tenentem: et catellam cingulo alligatam ducat: et cicaronem meum, et amphoras copiosas.

Satyricon 71

Vocabulary: *ponas*: you should place
tenens, tenentis: holding
catella -ae (f): little puppy
cingulo: to her belt
ducat: let her lead
cicaro, cicaronis (m): little boy

1. From the verb *alligo, alligare*, what does the form *alligatam* mean?

2. Say in Latin: "You [pl] should place statues of your parents [*parens*] holding our doves."

Post-Classical Latin Translation Practice

Biblia Vulgata, Hieronymus (347–420 PC)

"Nunc dimittis servum tuum, Domine, secundum verbum tuum, in pace, quia viderunt oculi mei salutare tuum, quod parasti ante faciem omnium populorum, lumen ad revelationem gentium et gloriam plebis tuae Israel."

Evangelium Secundum Lucam 2.29–32

Vocabulary: *in pace*: in peace
quia & *quod*: because
salutare, salutaris (n): salvation
parasti = *paravisti*
revelatio, revelationis (f): revelation

1. Check back on Lesson 6, and give the meaning of the prepositions *secundum* and *ante*.

2. What two translations are possible for the words *oculi mei*? Which will you choose, having carefully analyzed the clause the words appear in?

3. Give the reverse forms of the words *omnium populorum* and *plebis tuae* (*plebs*—20%).

Et dicebat: "Iesu, memento mei, cum veneris in regnum tuum."

Evangelium Secundam Lucam 23.42

Vocabulary: *memento* (imperative): be mindful, think!

1. Explain the form you see in *mei*. Give the reverse form.

2. In Lesson 6, what were the translations of the preposition *in* when it was followed by the object function?

3. Identify the time of the verb you see in *veneris*.

4. Say in Latin: "I will have come into your kingdoms."

Et ait ad illos: "Quis vestrum habebit amicum et ibit ad illum media nocte et dicet illi: 'Amice, commoda mihi tres panes.'"

Evangelium Secundam Lucam 11.5

Vocabulary:
ait: he said
ire: to go
media nocte: in the middle of the night
illi: to him
commodare: give
mihi: to me

1. Why is *vestrum*, rather than *vestri*, the proper form to use here?

2. Identify the verb time you see in *habebit*, *ibit* and dicet. Give the *ego* form for each verb, keeping the time the same.

3. What mood do you see in *commoda*? Give the B (legal or future) version of the same.

Dico autem <u>vobis</u>, <u>quod</u> nemo virorum <u>illorum</u>, qui vocati sunt, gustabit cenam meam.

Evangelium Secundam Lucam 14.24

Vocabulary: *vobis*: to you
quod: that
illorum: those

1. Which verb goes with *qui*, and who is the antecedent of *qui*?

2. What verb time and voice do you see in the two-word formula *vocati sunt*?

3. Say in Latin:

"The man who will have been called"

"The men who had been called"

"The women [*mulier*] who will call"

LESSON 21

THE OF-POSSESSION FUNCTION (GENITIVE) FOR THIRD-PERSON PRONOUNS

There is no possessive adjective to say *his, her, its,* or *their* in Latin.[1] Therefore the genitive of the pronoun (*is, ea, id*) is used for both uses (possession and feeling toward).

eius M/F/N	of him, of her, of it his, her, its **(meaning from context)**
eorum M/N	of them their
earum F	of them their

vidi eius filios in urbe.

I saw his sons in the city.

eorum milites in Galliam misit.

He sent their soldiers into Gaul.

desiderium eorum

Longing for them or *their longing*

1. The Latin word *suus -a -um,* which we will consider in Lesson 24, is something different; do not make assumptions about it for now.

Classical Latin Translation Practice

Marcus Cornelius Fronto (100–170 PC)

Maximi concursus ad audiendum eum Romae saepe facti sunt. Plurimi nostri ordinis viri facundiam eius non modo probant, sed etiam admirantur.

Epistulae ad Amicos

Vocabulary: *maximus -a -um*: very great
concursus (m pl subject): crowd
ad audiendum: to hear
Romae: at Rome
plurimus -a -um: very many
modo: only
admirantur: they marvel, admire

1. What verb time and voice do you recognize in the two-word formula *facti sunt*? Give two possible translations of that time. Give the two-word subject of that verb.

2. Reverse the words *nostri ordinis.*

3. Give the subject of *probant.*

4. Give six possible translations of *eius.* Which will you choose here, and why?

"In iis rebus et causis, quae a privatis iudicibus iudicantur, nullum inest periculum, quia sententiae eorum intra causarum demum terminos valent . . ."

Epistulae ad M. Caesarem

Vocabulary: *iis rebus et causis*: in these matters and cases
a privatis iudicibus: by private courts
iudicantur: [T.1 passive]
sententia -ae (f): decision
demum: only

1. Where in the dictionary do you find the verb *in-est*?

2. What is the antecedent of *quae*?

3. To whom does the *eorum* refer?

4. What function follows the preposition *intra*?

Duas per id tempus epistulas tuas accepi. Earum altera me increpabas et temere sententiam scripsisse arguebas, altera vero tueri studium meum laude nitebaris.

Epistulae ad M. Caesarem

Vocabulary: *per id tempus*: at the same time
altera . . . altera . . .: in the first . . . in the second . . .
temere: rashly
scripsisse: having written
arguere: to charge with
vero: but
tueri: to support
laude: with praise
nitebaris: you were making an effort

1. Translate the first sentence.

2. To what word does the pronoun *earum* refer? What translation for *earum* works here?

Omnes autem Ciceronis epistulas legendas censeo, mea sententia vel magis quam omnis eius orationes: Epistulis Ciceronis nihil est perfectius.

Epistulae ad M. Caesarem

Vocabulary: *legendus -a -um*: needing to be read
censere: I judge
mea sententia: in my opinion
vel magis quam: even more than
epistulis: than the letters
perfectius: more perfect

1. If the adjective *omnis* is here describing *orationes*, then what function is *omnis*? (Remind yourself of the alternative spelling of this function in the notes to Lesson 13.)

2. Give six possible translations of the word *eius*. Which works here and why?

Post-Classical Latin Translation Practice

Galileo Galilei (1564–1642 PC)

Praeclarum ... atque humanitatis plenum eorum fuit institutum, qui excellentium ... virorum res praeclare gestas ab invidia tutari, eorumque ... nomina ab oblivione atque interitu vindicare, conati sunt.

Sidereus Nuncius

Vocabulary: *institutus -a -um*: undertaken
res praeclare gestas (object): magnificent achievements
ab invidia: from envy
tutari: to defend
ab oblivione atque interitu: from oblivion and ruin
conati sunt: [they] have tried

1. What do you do to an adjective like *praeclarus*, when it is standing on its own in a sentence?

2. So what is a *praeclarum*? Which adjective describes it?

3. Which verb (given in the vocabulary) links with *qui*, and must be taken with both of the final phrases?

4. How do you translate the suffix *-que*, and where does it belong in the sentence when you translate it, in relation to the word it is attached to?

5. What two translations are possible for *eorum*? You will need them both here.

6. Give the reverse form of *nomina*.

Igitur in ipsa Luna et circa eius perimetrum multiplex est eminentiarum et cavitatum coordinatio. . . .

Sidereus Nuncius

Vocabulary: *eminentia -ae* (f): projection
cavitas, cavitatis (f): a hollow
coordinatio -onis (f): arrangement

1. Of the six possible translations of *eius*, which will you choose here and why?

Luna . . . albicantia cornua . . . ad nos convertit, et leviter Terram illustrat: crescit in Luna . . . Solaris illuminatio; augetur in terris eius luminis reflexio.

Sidereus Nuncius

Vocabulary: *albicans, albicantis*: whitening
cornu (n): a horn
leviter: lightly
in Luna: on the Moon
augetur: [T.1 passive (*augeo*)]
in terris: on the earth

1. Give the various singular subjects of *illustrat*, *crescit*, and *augetur*. What does this remind us about word order in Latin?

2. To what does the *eius* refer?

3. Reverse the words *eius luminis reflexio.*

In altero exemplo sex Stellas Tauri, PLEIADAS depinximus. [stellarum invisibilium] nos tantum triginta sex adnotavimus; earumque interstitia, magnitudines, necnon veterum novarumque discrimina, veluti in Orione, servavimus.

Sidereus Nuncius

Vocabulary: *in altero exemplo*: in another example
interstitium -i (n): the distance apart
necnon: and also
discrimen, discriminis (n): difference, distinction
veluti: just as
in Orione: in Orion's case

1. Say in Latin: "They painted the illumination [*illuminatio*] of the invisible star and preserved the size of an old and of a new star."

LESSON 22

THE PASSIVE VOICE IN TIMES 1-2-3

To work easily with the forms of Times 1-2-3 passive you need to have mastered the active forms (Lesson 12). Review for a moment:

dicam	T.3	*I shall say*
doceo	T.1	*I teach*
laudabas	T.2	*you were praising*
docebimus	T.3	*we will teach*
scribent	T.3	*they will write*
vocatis	T.1	*you call*
audiebat	T.2	*he/she/it was hearing*

There is a simple key to making these verb forms passive: identify the person ending and **flip it to the passive person ending**.

Subject of verb	*Active Person Ending*	*Passive Person Ending*
I	**-o**	**or**
	-m	**-r**
you	**-s**	**-ris**
he/she/it	**-t**	**-tur**
we	**-mus**	**-mur**
you	**-tis**	**-mini**
they	**-nt**	**-ntur**

dicar	T.3	*I shall be said*
doceor	T.1	*I am taught*
laudabaris	T.2	*you were being praised*
docebimur	T.3	*we will be taught*
scribentur	T.3	*they will be written*
vocamini	T.1	*you are summoned*
audiebatur	T.2	*he/she/it was being heard*

Two Exceptions

Time 1	Group 3 and Fence	**dicis** *you say*	>	**diceris** (not *diciris*) *you are said*
		capis *you capture*	>	**caperis** (not *capiris*) *you are captured*
Time 3	Group 1 and 2	**adiuvabis** *you will help*	>	**adiuvaberis** (not *adiuvabiris*) *you will be helped*
		delebis *you will destroy*	>	**deleberis** (not *delebiris*) *you will be destroyed*

Passive Traps

For Group 3 and Fence verbs, the T.1 you-singular passive form is now indistinguishable from the T.3 you-singular passive form, at least on paper. However, the *e* that displaces the expected *i* is **short in quantity, so the word would have different emphasis were you to say it out loud:**

T.1	**dīceris**	*you are said*
T.3	**dicēris**	*you will be said*

Where verbs have a PP3 stem that is identical to the PP1 stem, we have the added confusion of T.6 indicative active. Take the verb *extendo, extendere, extendi, extentus*:

extendis [T.1 active: you] becomes **extēnderis** (T.1 passive)—*you are stretched out*

extendes (T.3 active) becomes **extendēris** (T.3 passive)—*you will be stretched out*

T.6 active is **extēnderis**—*you will have stretched out*

Classical Latin Translation Practice

Publius Ovidius Naso (43 AC–18 PC)

Nam, quamquam sapor est adlata dulcis in unda,
gratius ex ipso fonte bibuntur aquae.

Epistulae ex Ponto 3.5.17–18

Vocabulary: *adlata in unda*: in water which has been fetched
gratius: more gratefully
ex ipso fonte: from the fountain itself

1. Say in Latin: "Waters were being drunk"; "Waters will be drunk."

parte tamen meliore mei super alta perennis
astra ferar, nomenque erit indelebile nostrum.

Metamorphoses 15.875–76

Vocabulary: *parte … meliore*: by means of the better part
fero, ferre [treat like Group 3]: carry

1. Which person do you see as the subject of the verbal form *ferar*? Give two possible translations for this verb.

2. Which adjective describes the subject of *ferar*? Give the reverse form.

3. What is special about the preposition *super*?

4. Reverse the last four words.

Quintus Horatius Flaccus (65 AC–8 PC)

cras donaberis haedo.

Carmina 3.13

Vocabulary: *donare*: to present
haedo: with a kid

1. What subject and time do you spot in *donaberis*?

2. Say in Latin: "We were being presented with a kid"; "They are presented"; "I will be presented."

Post-Classical Latin Translation Practice

10 Ergo dum nox erit dies,
et dum labor erit quies,
et dum aqua erit ignis,
et dum silva sine lignis,

11 Et dum mare sine velis,
et dum Parthus sine telis,
cara mihi semper eris:
nisi fallar, non falleris!

Carmina Burana 117

Vocabulary:
dum: until
sine lignis / velis / telis: without wood / sails / weapons
Parthus -i (m): the Parthian
mihi: to me

1. Given the verb *fallo*, *fallere*: to deceive, what is ambiguous about the form *falleris*? Explain, using an accent mark to show the difference in pronunciation for the different times.

Aurelius Augustinus (354–430 PC)

exhalabantur nebulae de limosa concupiscentia carnis et scatebra pubertatis, et obnubilabant atque obfuscabant cor meum.

Confessiones 2

Vocabulary: *de limosa concupiscentia . . . et scatebra*: out of the muddy desire and the bubbling up

1. What passive verb time do you see in the form *exhalabantur*? Give the T.1 and T.3 forms, keeping the subject the same.

2. Say in Latin: "My heart was being obscured."

ibam longius a te, et sinebas, et iactabar et effundebar et diffluebam et ebulliebam per fornicationes meas, et tacebas.

Confessiones 2

Vocabulary: *longius a te*: too far from you

1. Reverse all the verbs in the text.

tu non tacebas, et in illa contemnebaris a me.

Confessiones 2

Vocabulary: *in illa*: in her
a me: by me

1. Which person and time do you recognize in the passive form *contemnebaris*?

2. Give the T.1 and T.3 form of the verb, keeping the subject the same, and explain the consequent ambiguity. Solve the ambiguity by adding an accent mark.

ignorantia quoque ipsa . . . simplicitatis et innocentiae nomine tegitur.

Confessiones 2

Vocabulary: *ipse*, *ipsa*, *ipsum*: that very
nomine: under the name
tegere: to disguise

1. Say in Latin: "His ignorance was being and will be disguised."

LUDUS 7

AFTER LESSONS 19–22

Topics covered: the rest of the genitive; T.1-2-3 passive.

The first real "novel" or full-length adventure story that we have in Latin literature was written at the time of Nero (54–68 PC) by Gaius Petronius Arbiter "Elegantiarum" and is called the *Satyricon*, a medley of poetry and prose. In addition to being very funny, it is a goldmine of brilliant, colloquial Latin.

A.

A scene from the banquet at Trimalchio's house (which Fellini made into a great film in 1969!):

> **statim allatae sunt amphorae vitreae diligenter gypsatae, quarum in cervicibus pittacia erant affixa cum hoc titulo: "Falernum Opimianum annorum centum." dum titulos perlegimus, complosit Trimalchio manus et "eheu" inquit "ergo diutius vivit vinum quam homuncio. quare tangomenas faciamus. vinum vita est. verum Opimianum praesto. heri non tam bonum posui, et multo honestiores cenabant."**
>
> *Satyricon* 34.7

Vocabulary: *affero, afferre, attuli, allatum*: to bring in, deliver
diligenter: carefully
gypso (1): to plug, seal with plaster
in cervicibus: on the necks
pittacium -i (n): sticker, stamp, ticket
cum hoc titulo: with this inscription
complodere: clap-together
manus (object pl—Lesson 30): hands
diutius: longer
quam: (here) than

homuncio: little man
tangomena -ae (f) [derived from an unknown Greek word]: merriment, binge-drinking
Opimianus -a -um: from Opimius's vintage, c. 121 AC
praestare: to offer
multo honestiores: much more decent people

1. Where in your dictionary, after a certain search, do you find the verb *posui*?

2. What possible English meanings can we give to the Latin form *quarum*? Give two possible translations for *quarum in cervicibus*.

3. Explain the gender you see in *allatae* and *quarum*.

4. What is the difference between *inquit* (see dictionary under *inquam*) and *inquirit*?

5. What verb times do you see in lines 1 and 2? Explain fully.

6. Give the meaning of the following phrases:

   a. *vinum vita est proclamatum* ________________
   b. *vinum est vita* ________________
   c. *vinum est vita descripta* ________________

7. Translate the vivid text and imagine yourself down near Naples with Trimalchio's guests.

8. If the reversed form for *in cervicibus* is *in cervice*, reverse the whole first sentence up to *affixa*.

9. Write in Latin, "When [*cum*] your and their jars will have been brought into this banquet [*epulae -arum* (f) (used only in plural)], we shall dine as much finer people today than yesterday or tomorrow, because we little men shall be living longer than the wine which we shall have drunk [*bibo, bibere, bibi*]."

B.

1. In the class reading for Lesson 21, how did Fronto say: "Very many men of our order approve his eloquence"?

2. Write in Latin, using the same vocabulary but for different sentences:

   a. "His eloquence is approved and will be approved always among very many senators of my and their order."

   b. "Our eloquence had been approved and was being approved through the permanent [*permanens -entis* and *perpetuus -a -um*: use both Latin adjectives] scrutiny [*investigatio -onis* (f)] of our and her listeners [*auditor -oris* (m)]."

For over a thousand years the life, times, and deeds of Jesus of Nazareth have been read in Latin in the Biblia Vulgata. We've already translated several excerpts; here are some more examples.

C.

ubicumque fuerit corpus, <u>illuc</u> congregabuntur et aquilae.

Evangelium Secundum Matthaeum 24.28

Vocabulary: *illuc*: to that place

1. If the verb is *congrego* (1), then what time do you see hidden in the verb form in the text?

2. Give two different correct translations for that time.

3. Translate the line, giving special attention to the exact time of *fuerit* and the special meaning of *et* (Lesson 3).

4. Write out the Latin and English for Times 1, 2, and 5 of the verbs used in this sentence, keeping the subject the same.

D.

et veniunt in domum archisynagogi; et videt tumultum et flentes et eiulantes multum et ingressus ait eis: "quid turbamini et ploratis? puella non est mortua sed dormit." Et irridebant eum. . . . "Puella, tibi dico: surge!" Et confestim surrexit puella et ambulabat; erat enim annorum duodecim.

Evangelium Secundum Marcum
5.38–42

Vocabulary: *flens, flentis*: a person weeping
eiulans, eiulantis: a person howling
multum: [adverb in dictionary under *multus -a -um*]
ingressus -a -um: having entered
eis: to them
turbo (1): disturb
ploro (1): cry

1. What two possible meanings do you see in the first five words of the passage?

2. What voice is immediately suggested by the ending on *turbamini*? What is the reversed form?

3. What time is *turbamini*? Give T.4 for that verb, keeping the subject the same.

4. Translate the passage.

5. Focus on the second part of line 1 and write in Latin: "A tumult of people weeping and of people howling was being seen around him and his disciples [*discipulus -i* (m)], whose friendship [*amicitia -ae* (f)] the girl's parents were seeking [*peto, petere*]."

LESSON 23

THE FIRST- AND SECOND-PERSON REFLEXIVE PRONOUN (SUBJECT, OBJECT, AND OF-POSSESSION FUNCTIONS)

In Latin, a reflexive pronoun is a pronoun that reflects back on the subject of the sentence. It is not the subject; it reflects back on the subject.

I praise *myself*	is reflexive
You praise *me*	is not reflexive
They bring *their* books	may or may not be reflexive: it depends on whose the books are

The first- (*ego/nos*) and second- (*tu/vos*) person reflexive pronoun forms, and their possessive adjectives, *are identical to the first- and second-person pronoun forms already learned* (Lessons 3 and 20). If these pronouns refer back to the subject, you will know they are being used reflexively.

Object example:

nimis amas te

you love yourself too much

Of-possession example (using possessive adjective):

nimis lucra amabatis vestra

you used to love your profits too much

Sometimes you can also use the possessive adjective reflexively; sometimes it won't be reflexive.

vestras pecunias condidistis

you saved your money

vestras pecunias abstulerunt

they stole your money

Two Translation Practices

Marcus Tullius Cicero

sin eadem nos fortuna premet, etiamne reliquias tuas miseras proicies?

Ad Familiares 14.2

Vocabulary: *sin*: but if
idem, eadem, idem: the same
reliquiae, arum (f pl): remnants, leavings

1. Which word is reflexive: *nos* or *tuas*?

Augustinus

Nos diligimus quia ipse prior dilexit nos.

Sermo 34

LESSON 24

THE THIRD-PERSON REFLEXIVE PRONOUN (SUBJECT, OBJECT, AND OF-POSSESSION FUNCTIONS)

The third-person reflexive pronouns all begin with the letter "s." These unique s-words can be used only where the pronoun or possessive adjective is reflexive, that is, it refers back to, or reflects, the subject of the sentence. These "s-words" are used for all the third person, singular and plural, so are used for *him*, *her*, *it*, *one*, *them*, *his*, *her*, *its*, and *their*. They will therefore take their meaning from the subject of the verb.

Object form	**se**	*him, her, it (-self)* *them(selves)*
Possessive adjective (possessive, subjective)	**suus -a -um**	*his, her, its, their (own)*
Feeling toward (objective and partitive)	**sui**	*of him, of her, of it (-self)* *of them(selves)*

Sometimes you *must* use the s-word:

suam habet pecuniam Marcus

Marcus has his (own) money.

vident se

They see themselves.

Sometimes you *cannot* use the s-word:

eorum habet pecuniam Marcus

Marcus has their money.

videmus eos

We see them.

If the subject of the verb is *ego, tu, nos, vos,* you will see the pronoun *is, ea, id* used for anything to do with the third person. If the subject of the verb is *is, ea, id,* you will see either that pronoun or one of the s-words used for the third person, depending on whether the sentence is reflexive or not.

Like all adjectives, the possessive adjective *suus -a -um* must agree with the noun it is describing in terms of function, number, and gender. But it derives its meaning from the subject it reflects back on. The meaning of *suus -a -um* or *se* or *sui* depends on the subject of the sentence in which it is found. By contrast, the meaning of *eius* or *eorum / earum* will be determined by the context.

So in the English sentence "Paul jumped out of the window and saved his life," the use of *vitam suam* for "his life" would indicate that Paul saved his own life. The use of *vitam eius* would indicate that Paul jumped out of the window and saved someone else's life!

Classical Latin Translation Practice

Publius Ovidius Naso (43 AC–18 PC)

se cupit imprudens . . .
ista repercussae, quam cernis, imaginis umbra est:
nil habet ista sui; tecum venitque manetque; . . .
perque oculos perit ipse suos. . . .

Metamorphoses 3.425, 434, and 440

Vocabulary: *iste, ista, istud*: that
repercutio, repercutere, repercussi, repercussum: reflect
tecum: with you
ipse (m subject sing): he

1. If the subject of *cupit* is Narcissus, what does *se* mean in the first line?

2. In line 2, which word agrees with *umbra* and which word agrees with *imaginis*?

3. From the verb given, what must *repercussae* mean?

4. From the reflexive pronoun, what function do you see in *sui*? Give all the possible translations of that form. Which one are you going to choose here and why?

5. What are all the possible translations of *suus -a -um*? Which are you going to choose for *suos* in the final line?

Gaius Suetonius Tranquillus (c. 69–c. 126 PC)

atavus eius Cn. Domitius in tribunatu pontificibus offensior [erat], quod alium quam se in patris sui locum cooptassent.

De Vita Neronis 2

Vocabulary: *in tribunatu*: during his tribuneship
pontificibus: with the priests
offensior, offensioris: rather offended
quam: than
cooptassent: they had elected

1. Can *eius* refer to Domitius?

2. The *se* and *sui* do refer to Domitius. What function is each one? Is *sui* a possessive adjective, or a pronoun?

Icarus . . . iuxta cubiculum eius decidit ipsumque cruore respersit.

De Vita Neronis 12

Vocabulary: *ipsum*: him [Nero]
cruore: with blood

1. Why did the author not use *suus -a -um* in the phrase *cubiculum eius*?

2. In your list of prepositions that are followed by the object function (Lesson 6), what is the meaning of *iuxta*?

Cornelius Tacitus (56–120 PC)

hunc sui finem multos ante annos crediderat Agrippina contempseratque.

Annales 14.9

Vocabulary: *hunc* (m object sing): this

1. What things could *sui* be in a Latin sentence? What will you choose here and why?

2. Give the other five times of *crediderat* and *contempserat*, keeping the subject the same.

3. Say in Latin: "She will be believed"; "She was being despised."

Post-Classical Latin Translation Practice

Biblia Vulgata, Hieronymus (347–420 PC)

Mulierem fortem quis inveniet? . . . Accinxit fortitudine lumbos suos, et roboravit bracchium suum. Gustavit, et vidit quia bona est negotiatio eius; non exstinguetur in nocte lucerna eius. Manum suam misit ad fortia, et digiti eius apprehenderunt fusum. Manum suam aperuit inopi, et palmas suas extendit ad pauperem.

Liber Proverbiorum 31.10–20

Vocabulary:
fortitudine: with strength
quia: (here) that
in nocte: at night
manum [f object sing—Lesson 30]: hand
fusus -i (m): spindle
inopi: to/for the needy

1. Given the verb *exstinguo, exstinguere* (to put out, quench), what time and voice do you see in *exstinguetur*? Give the other five times, keeping the subject the same.

2. Explain why the text switches from *suos* and *suum* in the second sentence, to *eius* in the third sentence? Why do you find *suam* in the first half of the fourth sentence, but *eius* in the second half?

Et factum est, ut audivit salutationem Mariae Elisabeth, exsultavit infans in utero eius: et repleta est Spiritu Sancto Elisabeth: et exclamavit voce magna, et dixit: Benedicta tu inter mulieres, et benedictus fructus ventris tui. . . . Et ait Maria: Magnificat anima mea Dominum: et exsultavit spiritus meus in Deo salutari meo. Quia respexit humilitatem ancillae suae: ecce enim ex hoc beatam me dicent omnes generationes.

Evangelii Secundum Lucam 1.41

Vocabulary: *ut*: when
in utero eius: in her womb
Spiritu Sancto: with the Holy Spirit
voce magna: in a loud voice
in Deo salutari meo: in God my savior
ex hoc: from this

1. Why could the text use the possessive adjective *suus -a -um* in the last sentence, but use *eius* in the first sentence?

2. Is *tui* in this text reflexive?

"Omne regnum divisum contra se desolatur, et omnis civitas vel domus divisa contra se non stabit. Et si Satanas Satanam eicit, adversus se divisus est; quomodo ergo stabit regnum eius? Et si ego in Beelzebul eicio daemones, filii vestri in quo eiciunt? Ideo ipsi iudices erunt vestri."

Evangelium Secundum Matthaeum 12.25–7

Vocabulary: *dividere*: to divide
desolare: to abandon, devastate
Satanas, Satanae (m): Satan
eicere: to cast out
in Beelzebul: in the name of Beelzebub
in quo: in what, on what
ipsi: they themselves

1. When *vestri* is a possessive adjective, what does it mean? And when it's a pronoun? Give the reverse of each form.

2. From the verb *divido, dividere, divisi, divisus* (divide), what does the form *divisus -a -um* mean on its own? What happens to the meaning when you add *est*?

3. What is always ambiguous about *eius* in Latin? Here, what gender is *regnum*, and what gender is *eius*?

4. What is the difference in meaning, and why, between the *se* in the first sentence and the *se* in the second sentence?

5. What subject, verb time, and voice do you see in *desolatur*? Give the other five times, keeping the subject the same.

LESSON 25

THE ABLATIVE (BY-WITH-FROM-IN) FUNCTION IN NOUNS AND ADJECTIVES, AND WITH PREPOSITIONS

The ablative function is extremely rich in its application. There are about twenty-two formal uses of the ablative, but these can be condensed into four basic translations:

by
with
from
in

When you are translating the ablative function endings, try out each of these possible translations for size: at least one will work in almost all cases.

Block 1 Ablative Endings

	Masculine	*Feminine*	*Neuter*
Block 1 Word (Nouns and Adjectives)	**lup*us* -i** (m) **puer, pueri** (m) **magnus**	**capell*a* -ae** (f) **magna**	**aratr*um* -i** (n) **magnum**
Singular Ablative	**-o**	**-a**	**-o**
Plural Ablative	**-is**	**-is**	**-is**

The *by-with-from-in* ending for feminine singular nouns causes a big problem here. Although the ablative *-a* is actually long in quantity—so you can hear a difference, especially in metrical poetry—it is identical on paper to the subject singular ending. Take the sentence: *pecunia me servavit.* This is ambiguous, as *pecunia* could be subject singular ("money preserved me") or ablative singular ("he/she/it preserved me with money").

The Block 1 *by-with-from-in* plural is identical to the Block 2 of-possession function singular. The only solution to this possible difficulty is to know where the word comes from in the dictionary.

Block 2 Ablative Endings

	Nouns	*Adjectives*
Block 2 Word	**rex, regis** (m)	**acer, acris, acre**
Singular Ablative	**-e / -i** 80/20	**-i / -e** 80/20
Plural Ablative	**-ibus**	**-ibus**

rex illustris imperatoris sui ingentibus copiis urbem oppugnavit.
The king attacked the city with the vast forces of his famous commander.

or

The famous king attacked the city with the vast forces of his commander.

Prepositions Followed by the Ablative Function

A preposition describes where things are in relation to each other. We learned, in Lesson 6, about the four "special" prepositions. These are always followed by the ablative funtion-case when **no sense of motion** (physical or moral) is indicated.

These four prepositions are special because, when there *is* a sense of motion involved (i.e., when they describe a movement or attitude toward something), they are followed by the object (accusative) function.

The Four Special Prepositions

in	in, on
sub	under
subter	under
super	above

Other Prepositions Followed by the Ablative

a, ab, abs	by (when expressing *by whom* something is done) from, away from (when expressing ideas of space and time)
absque	without
coram	in the presence of, face to face
cum	with (when expressing accompaniment, *not* instrumentality)
de	down from, away from, about, concerning, in respect to
e, ex	out of, from the middle of, since, according to
prae	in front of, in preference to, before, because of, for
pro	before, in front of, as good as, in proportion to, by virtue of, instead of, in favor of, in accordance with, in return for, on behalf of . . .
sine	without
tenus	as far as, up to (extent) (also can be followed by the genitive)

Note how many of these prepositions have multiple meanings. These translations are by no means exhaustive!

It is important to note that when you express *by whom* something is done, for example with a passive verb, and the agent is a person, you must use the preposition *a*, *ab*, *abs*. However, when you are expressing the means by which something is done, for instance, traveling "by boat" or building "with bricks," you use the ablative on its own. This is called the *ablative of instrument*.

NB: Prepositions are normally placed before the word they govern (but not necessarily next to it!).

Some Illustrations of the Ablative Function and Its Four Basic Meanings in Various Uses

- Place from where one is coming: ***e / ex + ablative***

  redeo ex urbe

  I return from the city

- Origin from whom something comes: ***a / ab / abs + ablative***

  accepi litteras meo a patre

  I received a letter from my father

  emere aliquid ab aliquo

  To buy something from somebody

- Separation: ***a / ab /abs + ablative*** for a person; **ablative alone** for a thing

  patriam ab hostibus liberavit

  He freed the country from enemies

  patriam servitute liberavit

  He freed the country from slavery

- Agent *by whom* something is done: ***a / ab / abs + ablative***

  amor meis a parentibus
  I am loved by my parents

- Instrument *by which* something is done: **ablative alone**

  ferire gladio
  To strike with a sword

  equo vehi
  To be conveyed by horse

  diluere aqua vinum
  To temper wine with water

- Cause because of which something happens: **ablative alone**

  fama interiit
  He died from hunger

- Manner in which something is done: **ablative alone**

  magna voce exclamat

  He cries out in a loud voice

- Accompaniment: ***cum + ablative***

  cum amico cenabam
  I was dining with a friend

- Description in what way:

  voce absoni
  Grating in voice

LESSON 26

THE ABLATIVE FUNCTION IN PRONOUNS

The pronouns in the ablative case [function] are shown in the following chart:

Pronoun	*Singular*	*Plural*
First Person *ego / nos*	**me** *by-with-from me*	**nobis** *by-with-from us*
Second Person *tu / vos*	**te** *by-with-from you*	**vobis** *by-with-from you*
Third Person *is / ea / id*	**eo, ea, eo** *by-with-from him/her/it*	**eis** or **iis** *by-with-from them*
Third-Person Reflexive Pronoun *s-words*	**se** *by-with-from him/her/it*	**se** *by-with-from them*
Relative Pronoun *qui / quae / quod*	**quo, qua, quo** *by-with-from whom/ which*	**quibus** *by-with-from whom/ which*

The prepositions are normally placed before the word they govern (but not necessarily next to it!). An exception is *cum*, when it is used with many person pronouns. *Cum* is joined onto the pronoun as a suffix: with me = *mecum*; with you = *tecum*; with us = *nobiscum*; with you = *vobiscum*; with him/her/it/themselves = *secum*; with whom/ which = *quacum*, *quibuscum*.

quocum venistis?

with whom did you come?

sunt epistulae a nobis missae
the letters were sent by us

regina pro se dicebat
the queen was speaking on her own behalf

quid pro quo
something in return for something

[condicio] sine qua non
a condition without which not (possible)

Classical Latin Translation Practice

Gaius Plinius Caecilius Secundus (61–c. 113 PC)

In itinere quasi solutus ceteris curis, huic uni vacabat: ad latus notarius cum libro et pugillaribus, cuius manus hieme manicis muniebantur ... qua ex causa Romae quoque sella vehebatur.

Epistulae 3.5.15

Vocabulary: *quasi*: as if
huic uni: for this one (occupation)
manus (subject pl): hands
manicae, manicarum (f pl): long-sleeves, gloves
Romae: at Rome

1. Give the reason for the ablative endings of: *itinere*, *libro*, *pugillaribus*, and *qua causa*.

2. Who is the antecedent of *cuius*? Which verb must go with *cuius*?

3. From the verb *solvo, solvere* (free, release), what does *solutus* mean?

4. From the natural ablative meanings *by*, *with*, *from*, and *in*, think carefully about the context and pick the one that works best for *ceteris curis*, *hieme*, *manicis*, and *sella*.

Interim e Vesuvio monte pluribus locis latissimae flammae altaque incendia relucebant, quorum fulgor et claritas tenebris noctis excitabatur.

Epistulae 6.16.13

Vocabulary: *plures, plura*: rather many
latissimus -a -um; very broad
excitare: enliven, enhance

1. Identify the verb in the relative clause and the main verb.

2. What is the antecedent of *quorum*? Which of the three available translations for *quorum* will work best here?

3. What do the words *tenebris noctis* teach us about the difficulty of ablative endings?

Publius Vergilius Maro (70–19 AC)

Sum pius Aeneas, raptos qui ex hoste Penates
classe veho mecum, fama super aethera notus.

Aeneid 1.378

Vocabulary: *Penates, Penatium* (m pl): household gods

1. From the verbs *rapio, rapere* (snatch) and *nosco, noscere* (know) what do *raptos* and *notus* mean? Which noun does each one describe?

2. Explain the fusion of words you see in *me-cum*.

3. Mark off the relative clause here from the main clause (*raptos* belongs inside the relative clause).

4. What is the reason for the ablative *hoste*?

5. From the natural ablative meanings *by*, *with*, *from*, and *in*, think carefully about the context and pick the one that works best for *classe* and *fama*.

6. Reverse the last four words of the quoted passage.

Post-Classical Latin Translation Practice

Liturgia Romana, Paulus VI (1897–1978 PC)

Libera nos, quaesumus, Domine, ab omnibus malis,
da propitius pacem in diebus nostris,
ut, ope misericordiae tuae adiuti,
et a peccato simus semper liberi
et ab omni perturbatione securi:
exspectantes beatam spem
et adventum Salvatoris nostri Iesu Christi.

"Ritus Communionis"

Vocabulary: *ut*: so that
simus: we might be
exspectans, exspectantis: awaiting

1. What mood do you see in the verbs *libera* and *da*? Give the reverse form, and the object of each verb.

2. With whom do the adjectival forms *adiuti, liberi, securi,* and *exspectantes* agree?

3. Thinking about the four basic meanings for the ablative function, select the best translation for *ab omnibus malis, in diebus nostris, ope adiuti, a peccato liberi, ab perturbatione securi.*

INNOCENTIUS VI (1282–1362 PC)

Ave verum corpus, natum
de Maria Virgine,
vere passum, immolatum
in cruce pro homine
cuius latus perforatum
fluxit aqua et sanguine:
esto nobis praegustatum
in mortis examine.

"Ave verum corpus"

Vocabulary: *natus -a -um*: born
vere: truly
passus -a -um: having suffered
nobis: for us
praegustatum: a foretaste
examen, examinis (n): test, weighing

1. What is potentially misleading about the words *corp-us* and *lat-us*?

2. From the verbs *immolo, immolare* (to sacrifice) and *perforo, perforare* (to pierce), what do the forms *immolatum* and *perforatum* mean? Identify the noun each principal part is describing.

3. Box off the relative clause in this hymn. Who or what is the antecedent of *cuius*? What are the three possible translations of that word?

4. What mood do you spot in *esto*? Give the reverse form and the "they" form.

5. What is ambiguous about *aqua*? How would you go about solving the ambiguity?

6. Which noun is the object of *in* (line 8)?

Thomas Aquinus (1225–1274)

In <u>supremae</u> nocte cenae
<u>Recumbens</u> cum fratribus . . .
Cibum <u>turbae</u> <u>duodenae</u>
Se dat suis manibus.

"Pange lingua gloriosi"

Vocabulary: *supremus -a -um*: last
recumbens, recumbentis: reclining, sitting down
turbae duodenae: to the group of twelve

1. Of all the possible translations for *se* and *suus -a -um*, which are you going to choose here and why?

2. What noun is the object of the first word, *in*?

3. Of the natural translations available for the ablative, which are you going to choose for *suis manibus*?

LUDUS 8

AFTER LESSONS 23–26

Topics covered: the reflexive pronoun; the ablative case [function] for nouns, adjectives, and pronouns.

A.

Reginaldus Foster (1939–2020)

Tuis octavum verbis si ludum inceperis Latinis, magna a te percipietur studiorum hodie Latinorum utilitas multaque simul cum animi et mentis voluptate exerceberis ac delectaberis de caelo a Deo transmissa consolatione.

Ludus Domesticus

Vocabulary: *incipio, incipere, incepi, inceptum*: begin
simul: at the same time
exercēre: to exercise
delectare (1): to delight
transmitto, transmittere, transmisi, transmissum: to transmit, send over

1. Give the exact meaning for the verb forms here:

a. *delectaberis* ____________________

b. *inceperis* ____________________

c. *exerceberis* ____________________

2. Now give the reversed form for each of those verbs.

3. Look carefully at the following verb forms and point out the difference in time and voice between *incipieris* and *inceperis*. Reverse each verb form.

4. What is the difficulty presented by a superficial reading of *mentis* (*mens* = mind) and *verbis* (*verbum* = word). Reverse each word (*mens* is one of the 20%).

5. When do we use the preposition *cum* in Latin? What does it mean?

6. What is the difference between *ad Deum* and *a Deo*? Reverse both phrases.

7. Which different meanings can be attached to the function-case of *transmissa consolatione*?

8. Translate the phrase of Reginaldus.

We are now mature enough in Latin to deal with some full, solid Latin of one of the few Roman-born writers of Latin literature—Gaius Julius Caesar (102–44 AC)—in his immortal *Commentarii*, a continuation of a reading in Lesson 22. After Caesar crossed the Rubicon, his rival, Pompeius, invokes the Senate in Rome.

B.

omnes, qui sunt eius ordinis, a Pompeio evocantur. laudat promptos Pompeius atque in posterum [tempus] confirmat, segniores castigat atque incitat. multi undique ex veteribus Pompei exercitibus spe praemiorum atque ordinum evocantur, multi ex duabus legionibus, quae sunt traditae a Caesare, arcessuntur. conpletur urbs et ipsum comitium tribunis, centurionibus, evocatis. omnes amici consulum, necessarii Pompei atque ii, qui veteres inimicitias cum Caesare gerebant, in senatum coguntur. quorum vocibus et concursu terrentur infirmiores, dubii confirmantur.

Bellum Civile 1.3

Vocabulary:
ordo, ordinis (m): rank, order, social group
evocare (1): to summon, call out
promptus -a -um: ready, willing
posterus -a -um: following, later
segnior, segnioris: more lazy, more sluggish person
exercitibus (ablative pl—Lesson 30): armies
spe (ablative sing—Lesson 30): hope
tradere: to hand over, surrender
arcessere: to call, summon
complēre: to fill
ipse, ipsa, ipsum: self, the very
comitium -ii (n): the voting area in front of the senate
evocatus -i (m): recalled soldier
necessarius -i (m): relative, blood relation, close friend
gerere: to carry, harbor, administer
cogere: to force, drive
concursu (ablative sing): running together, concourse
infirmior, infirmioris: a weaker person

1. What two meanings do we attach to the Latin form *eorum*?

2. What translations are possible for *quorum*?

3. What meanings do we give the Latin form *eius* (list all)?

4. What is the difference between *sunt* in line 1 and *sunt* in line 4?

5. Keeping the same subject, give the other five indicative times for *sunt traditae*.

6. What function-case do you see in *vocibus*? Reverse that form.

7. What difficulty is presented by the adjacent words *necessarii Pompei*?

8. Think carefully about the simple Latin sentence *sunt amici quorum vocibus terremur* before rendering it in English. Give two possible translations.

9. What is the difference a well-trained Latinist will see between *completur urbs centurionibus* and *completur urbs ab centurionibus*?

10. Now translate the entire passage.

11. Make up some short Latin phrases quickly:

    a. On behalf of y'all and of Caesar's daughter.

    b. Many good things from a good girl [four Latin words]

    c. You are being summoned without wild animals [*fera -ae* (f)] but you will be soon be summoned in tattered [*lacerus -a -um*] cloaks [*lacerna -ae* (f)].

C.

Caesar talks about a Gallic chieftain, a friend of the Romans

Erat in Carnutibus summo loco natus Tasgetius, cuius maiores in sua civitate regnum obtinuerant. huic Caesar pro eius virtute atque in se benevolentia, quod in omnibus bellis singulari eius opera fuerat usus, maiorum locum restituerat.

De Bello Gallico 5.25

Vocabulary: *Carnutes -um* (m pl Block 2): the Carnutians
locus -i (m): position, level, status
nasco, nascere: bear (a child), give birth
maior, maioris: greater, ancestor
obtinere: to hold, occupy
huic: to this man
quod: (here) because
opera -ae (f): effort, diligence
utor, uti, usus sum: to use [+ object in the ablative]
restituere: to restore

1. In Lesson 25, what was pointed out about the meaning of prepositions? This means you have to be thoughtful about which meaning to assign to *pro* …

2. When you see *eius* in a Latin sentence, where do you look for its meaning?

3. When you see *suus -a -um* or *se*, where do you look for its meaning?

4. To whom does the *civitate* belong?

5. To whom does the *virtute* NOT belong?

6. What does *sua* mean in line 1? So why is it feminine singular?

7. Translate the passage.

LESSON 27

DEPONENT VERBS

There is a large group of verbs in Latin whose principal parts in the dictionary appear to be passive. The meaning of their PPs is the same as those for all other verbs. The theme vowels of the groups remain the same and are still visible, just as they are in the passive forms of normal verbs. We can characterize a "v.dep" as a verb that looks passive in the dictionary but is translated with an active meaning.

Deponent Verbs in the Dictionary

Group and Theme Vowel	*PP1 T.1 ego*	*PP2 Infinitive*	*PP3 T.4 ego*	*Meaning*
Group 1: a	**gratulor** *I congratulate*	**gratulari** *to congratulate*	***gratulatus* sum** *I have congratulated* *I congratulated*	congratulate
Group 2: strong e	**fateor**	**fateri**	***fassus* sum**	confess
Group 3: weak e	**sequor**	**sequi**	***secutus* sum**	follow
Group 4: i	**orior**	**oriri**	***ortus* sum**	arise
Fence/Mixed Verbs	**patior**	**pati**	***passus* sum**	suffer

These verbs are called "deponent" (*verbum deponens*) from the Latin verb *depono, deponere, deposui, depositus -a -um*, meaning "to put down or lay aside." This is because they have put aside half of their nature: they have put aside the possibility of having active forms and of having passive meaning.

Notes

- From study, reading, and Latin experience you will, and must, get to know these verbs sooner or later. Know your vocabulary!
- One thing to look out for as a clue to the fact you might be reading a deponent verb is the presence of an object form. Remember, **there is no direct object with a true passive verb.**
- What happens if you want to say something in the passive voice with one of these verbs? You cannot! For example, all of the verbs for "to follow" in Latin are deponent. You cannot say, verbatim, in Latin, "the laws were being followed." You would have to find a circumlocution.
- PP2 has the appearance of the passive infinitive. Notice how most groups' passive infinitive just ends in an *i* instead of an *e*. However, the passive infinitive of Group 3 verbs is particularly deceptive and easy to miss, being so short: *sequi*, *pati*.
- PP3 is T.4. However, when you remove *sum* from that formula, you are left with the past participle. This works in the same way as PP4 for normal verbs, except that the participle here is **active**. Therefore, the italicized words in the chart mean, on their own, not "having been" but: *having congratulated*, *having confessed*, *having followed*, *having arisen*, and *having suffered*.

pueri turbam puellarum sequebantur

The boys were following the crowd of girls.

trapezita pecunias largietur

The money-changer will give out money generously.

laudes meremur

We merit praises.

haec semper loquimini

You always say these things.

trivit auriga suos terribiles hortatus equos metam.

The charioteer having spurred on his terrible horses grazed the turning post.

Classical Latin Translation Practice

Gaius Sallustius Crispus (86–35 AC)

quae quousque tandem patiemini, o fortissumi viri? nonne emori per virtutem praestat quam vitam miseram atque inhonestam ... per dedecus amittere?

Bellum Catilinae 20.9

Vocabulary: *quae* [connecting relative pronoun]: these things
quousque: up to what point
fortissumus -a -um: bravest
praestat: it is better
quam: (here) than
amittere: to lose

1. From the deponent verb *patior, pati, passus sum* (suffer), what verb time and subject do you identify in the form *patiemini*?

2. What is the function of *quae* in the first sentence?

3. From the deponent verb *emorior, emori, emortuus sum* (die), what is the meaning of *emori*?

4. Remind yourself of question words (Lesson 18). What sort of answer does a question beginning with *nonne* expect?

Quin igitur expergiscimini? en illa, illa quam saepe optastis libertas, praeterea divitiae, decus, gloria in oculis sita sunt; ... res, tempus, pericula, egestas, belli spolia magnifica magis quam oratio mea vos hortantur. vel imperatore vel milite me utimini ...

Bellum Catilinae 20.14

Vocabulary: *quin*: why not?
optastis = *optavistis*
situs -a -um: placed, situated
magis quam: more than
vel ... vel ...: either ... or ...
utor, uti, usus sum + object in ablative: use

Do not be surprised by long lists of subjects without a conjunction!

1. From the verb *hortor, hortari* (encourage), what verb time and subject do you identify in *hortantur*? What is special about this kind of verb? Explain fully. Give the other five times in Latin, keeping the subject the same.

2. What time and subject do you see in *expergiscimini* and *utimini*?

3. In the second phrase, which verb links with *quam* and which is the main verb? Identify the antecedent of *quam*.

4. Leaving *vel ... vel ...* the same, reverse the last six words.

Pro his nos habemus luxuriam atque avaritiam, publice egestatem, privatim opulentiam. Laudamus divitias, sequimur inertiam. Inter bonos et malos discrimen nullum, omnia virtutis praemia ambitio possidet.

Bellum Catilinae 52.22

Vocabulary: *his* (ablative plural): these
publice: generally
privatim: individually

1. How can *sequimur* look so different from *habemus* and *laudamus*, and yet be translated in a similar way?

2. Which of its many meanings works best for *pro* here?

3. What do you do to the adjectives-on-their-own *bonos* and *malos* to bring out their meaning fully?

4. Reverse the last sentence.

Post-Classical Latin Translation Practice

Carolus Egger (1914–2003 PC)

Vaccae, ceteroqui praedicabiles, si … malum nanciscuntur, periculum possunt intendere homini.

Diarium Latinum, "'Insanae Vaccae' Britannicae Homines Territant"

Vocabulary: *intendere*: to threaten
homini: upon humans

1. What is unusual about the verb *nanciscuntur*? Give the other five times in Latin, keeping the subject the same.

2. Reverse the entire sentence, keeping *ceteroqui*, *si*, and *intendere homini* the same.

Iosuc Carlisle, puerulus decem annorum, ex horto patriae domus . . . clam exiit, sequi cupiens, ut videtur, duos sine domino canes erraticos, qui in vicinia vagabantur. Imprudens parvulus in silvam se intulit, unde se expedire non valuit.

Diarium Latinum, "Duo Canes Erratici Puerulum Servant a Morte"

Vocabulary: *patrius -a -um*: belonging to a father
domus: of the home
exeo, exire, exii: to go out, leave
cupiens, cupientis: eager
ut: as
videor, videri, visus sum: seem, appear
parvulus -i (m): child, little boy
valeo, valere, valui: to have strength, power

1. From the verb *sequor, sequi, secutus sum* (follow), what must the form *sequi* mean?

2. Upon which subject do the pronouns *se* reflect back?

3. Explain the ablative ending you see in *horto, domino, vicinia.* Bring out the clear difference in meaning between *in vicinia* and *in silvam.*

4. Which verb must link with *qui*? What is the antecedent of *qui*?

Non solum publici custodes sed etiam plurimi cives voluntarii omnia sunt scrutati, omnia circumspexerunt, nec tamen vestigium parvuli ullum apparuit.

Diarium Latinum, "Duo Canes Erratici Puerulum Servant a Morte"

Vocabulary: *plurimus -a -um*: very many

1. In the parallel phrases *omnia sunt scrutati* and *omnia circumspexerunt*, how can the verbs look so different but be translated in a similar way? Which five words constitute the subject of each verb?

2. How do you bring out the meaning of *omnia* fully?

Tandem unus e voluntariis, silvam perlustrans, ad latratum caninum aures erexit, animum attendit estque hoc persecutus indicium.

Diarium Latinum, "Duo Canes Erratici Puerulum Servant a Morte"

Vocabulary: *perlustrans, perlustrantis*: wandering through
erigere: to prick up
animum attendere: to apply the mind, direct the attention
hoc (neuter): this

1. Give the seven possible translations of *attendit*.

2. Which will you choose in this context, keeping in mind the other verb in the line *est persecutus*?

3. Say in Latin: "Although [*quamquam*] we had pursued the barking of a dog, we were finding no signs of him [the boy]."

LESSON 28

THE DATIVE FUNCTION (TO-FOR-FROM) IN NOUNS, ADJECTIVES, AND PRONOUNS

The dative has three natural translations:

to, *for*, or *from*

The word "dative" comes from the verb *do*, *dare*, *dedi*, *datus*, "give." You can hear the **indirect object** with this verb: I gave a present *to* my brother, but the other translations (*for* and *from*) are also common as indirect objects: I bought a present *for* my brother; my brother snatched the present *from* me.

Block 1 Dative Endings

Block 1 Nouns and Adjectives	**lup*us* -i** (m) **magnus**	**capell*a* -ae** (f) **magna**	**aratr*um* -i** (**n**) **magnum**
Singular Dative	**-o**	**-ae**	**-o**
Plural Dative	**-is**	**-is**	**-is**

We have met all of these endings already. The feminine dative singular is identical to the feminine subject plural and feminine genitive singular. The dative plural is the same as the ablative plural.

Block 2 Dative Endings

Block 2 Nous and Adjectives	**rex, regis** (m) **acer, acris, acre**
Singular Dative	**-i**
Plural Dative	**-ibus**

Here again the dative singular could be confused with the ablative, especially with adjectives (80%), and the dative plural is identical to the ablative.

So, how do you distinguish the dative? **Hint: Look at the verb.** Many verbs invite the translation *to* or *for* or *from*. In addition, there are sixty-five verbs [henceforth known as "the 65"] that are automatically followed by the dative, where you would expect a direct object in the accusative (e.g., *faveo puero*, "I favor or I am well disposed towards the child"). A good dictionary will include "with dat." in the entry for these verbs.

Compound verbs are also frequently followed by the dative. Here, you will find common prepositions that normally have their own object, such as *ad*, *ante*, *circum*, *in*, *inter*, *ob*, *post*, *prae*, *sub*, and *super*, fixed onto the front of verbs. The original object of the preposition may now be found in the dative case [function], translated with the meaning of the preposition.

omnibus Druidibus praeest unus

one man presides over all Druids.

The Dative (To-For-From) Function in All Pronouns

The pronouns in the dative case can be found in the chart below:

Pronoun	*Singular*	*Plural*
First Person *ego / nos*	**mihi** *to-for-from me*	**nobis** *to-for-from us*
Second Person *tu / vos*	**tibi** *to-for-from you*	**vobis** *to-for-from you*
Third Person *is / ea / id*	**ei** *to-for-from him / her / it*	**eis** or **iis** *to-for-from them*
Third-Person Reflexive Pronoun *s-words*	**sibi** *to-for-from him / her / it*	**sibi** *to-for-from them*
Relative Pronoun *qui / quae / quod*	**cui** *to-for-from whom / which*	**quibus** *to-for-from whom / which*

ecclesiae sanctae

the holy churches **OR** *of the holy church* **OR** *for the holy church* **OR** *to the holy church?*

When in doubt always look at the verb:

omnia bona ecclesiae sanctae dedit.

He gave all his property to the holy church.

ecclesiae sanctae laetantur.

The holy churches rejoice.

ecclesiae sanctae auctoritatem imminuit.

He diminished the authority of the holy church.

ab omni discrimine patriam liberavit.

He freed the fatherland from every crisis.

omni civi nummos tribuit princeps.

The ruler granted coins to every citizen.

mihi nomen est Ioannes.

The name to me is John [*my name is John*].

cenam eis dedit mater.

The mother gave them dinner.

milites quibus arma hostes ademerant fugerunt.

The soldiers from whom the enemies had taken the weapons fled.

duo sues sibi emit puella.

The girl bought two pigs for herself.

Classical Latin Translation Practice

Cornelius Tacitus (56–120 PC)

sed ut haesere caeno fossisque impedimenta, turbati circum milites, incertus signorum ordo, utque tali in tempore sibi quisque properus et lentae adversum imperia aures, inrumpere Germanos iubet.

Annales 1.65

Vocabulary: *ut*: when
circum: [adverb here]
signum -i (n): military standard

1. Do not be surprised if in the second, third, and fourth phrases, you have to supply one or more parts of the verb "to be."

2. What shortened form of a specific verb time do you see in the form *haesere* (Lesson 8)? What must be the subject of that verb?

3. If each *ut* introduces a subordinate clause, what is the main verb in the sentence? What rule about reading Latin sentences does this remind us of?

4. From the verb *turbo, turbare*, what does *turbati* mean on its own? What happens to the meaning if you combine it with the verb *sunt*?

5. What is the meaning of the prepositional phrase *tali in tempore*, and what is pleasing about its style?

6. In the second *ut* clause there are two subjects, each the subject of an invisible part of "to be." Name them.

7. Of the all the possible translations, which one are you going to select for *sibi* here and why?

postquam haesere munimentis, datur cohortibus <u>signum</u> cornuaque ac tubae <u>concinuere</u>. <u>exim</u> clamore et <u>impetu</u> tergis Germanorum circumfunduntur.

Annales 1.68

Vocabulary: *signum -i* (n): signal
concino, concinere, concinui: sound together
exim: after that, then
impetu (ablative sing): attack, charge

1. Which shortened form of the verb do you see in *concinuere*? Give the reverse form.

2. With which preposition is the verb *fundere* compounded in the text? What is special about some compound verbs? Explain fully.

illum numine deum destinari credebant, fovebantque multi, quibus nova et ancipitia praecolere avida et plerumque fallax ambitio est.

Annales 14.22

Vocabulary: *ille, illa, illud*: he, she, it
deum = *deorum*
fovere: to support
anceps, ancipitis: hazardous

1. Looking ahead, can you work out the meaning of *destinari* from the verb *destino, destinare* (to destine, appoint). Use the table in Lesson 27 to help you.

2. What is the meaning of the suffix *-que*? Where does it belong in the sentence when you translate it, in relation to the word it is attached to?

3. What are the various ambiguities of the ending on *nova* and *ancipitia* and *avida*? Knowing which block *ancipitia* is in should help you work out which two adjectives are the object of *praecolere* and which describe the subject of the relative clause…

Post-Classical Latin Translation Practice

ARCHIPOETA (C. 1130–C. 1165 PC)

lingua balbus, hebes ingenio,
viris doctis sermonem facio.
sed quod loquor, qui loqui nescio,
necessitas est, non praesumptio.

Poem 1

Vocabulary: *ingenium -ii* (n): ability, natural talent
doctus -a -um: learned

1. What was the very first rule you learned about Latin word order? Therefore which word would you never presume to start translating from, or make assumptions about?

2. What is the missing pronoun antecedent of *quod*?

3. And who must be the antecedent of *qui*?

excitata vox praeconum
clamat viris regionum
advenire virum bonum,
patrem pacis et patronum,
cui Vienna parat tronum.

Poem 2

Vocabulary: *praeco, praeconis* (m): herald

1. From the verb *excitare* (to waken, rouse), what does *excitata* mean?

2. Which verb links with *cui*? Who is the antecedent of *cui*? Give the two possible translations for that relative pronoun.

3. Reverse the first two lines.

vir virorum optime, parce tuo vati,
qui se totum subicit tuae voluntati;

Poem 4

Vocabulary: *optime*: O most excellent
parco, parcere [+ dative]: to spare
totum: completely
sub+icio, sub+icere: to place under, submit

1. What is a good strategy when you think a word might be dative? Explain fully how the two verbs in these lines prove this point.

1. Who is the antecedent of *qui*?

3. What is the function and meaning of *se*?

ibi pulchritudinem vidi domus dei,
ipsum tamen oculi non videre mei;
nam divinae tantus est splendor faciei,
quod mirantur angeli, qui ministrant ei.

Poem 5

Vocabulary: *domus* (genitive): of the house
ipsum (object): [God] himself
faciei (f genitive): of the face
quod: that

1. Of what verb time is *videre* a short form? What is the subject of *videre*? Why is *videre* potentially such a confusing form?

2. What is special about the verb *mirantur*?

3. Which verb links with *qui* and what is the antecedent of *qui*? What is the function of *qui* in its own phrase?

4. What two different functions can *ei* be? (See also Lesson 3) Which are you going to choose here, and to whom does the pronoun refer?

5. Say in Latin: "The women, who will have attended to you, will marvel!"

LESSON 29

EXPRESSING COMMANDS USING PASSIVE AND DEPONENT VERBS

The passive imperative forms of normal verbs and the imperative forms of deponent verbs look the same. True passive imperatives will sound passive; deponent imperatives will sound active. True passive imperatives are rather rare.

Type A: The Present Imperative (Normal)

Commanding	*Group 1*	*Group 2*	*Group 3*	*Group 4*
tu (looks like PP2 of normal verbs)	**eradicare!** *be eradicated!*	**monere!**	**imponere!**	**invenire!**
	laetare! *rejoice!*	**confitere!**	**sequere!**	**largire!**
vos (identical to T.1 you-plural)	**eradicamini!**	**monemini!**	**regimini!**	**audimini!**
	hortamini!	**pollicemini!**	**ingredimini!**	**largimini!**

The singular passive imperative is identical to an active infinitive PP2 (ouch!). For a deponent verb, identify the group and *imagine* what the active infinitive would look like for that group. If *conor, conari, conatus sum* is a Group 1 verb, the active infinitive, if it existed, would be *conare*! Which, therefore, can only mean *try*!

Type B: The Future / Legal / Comic / Biblical Imperative

Commanding	*Group 1*	*Group 2*	*Group 3*	*Group 4*
tu **is, ea, id** (-*o* becomes -*or*)	**eradicator!**	**monetor!**	**imponetor!**	**largitor!**
vos [does not exist]	X	X	X	X
ei/eae/ea (-*nto* > -*ntor*)	**laudantor!**	**confitentor!**	**imponuntor!**	**erudiuntor!**

These are very rare!

mundare!	*be purified!*
largire!	*grant!*
me sequimini!	*follow me!*

Classical Latin Translation Practice

Publius Vergilius Maro (70–19 AC)

ergo age, care pater, cervici imponere nostrae;
ipse subibo umeris nec me labor iste gravabit.

Aeneid 2.707

Vocabulary: *age*: come on!
care: dear
imponere [*in+ pono*]: place on, set on
ipse: I myself
iste, ista, istud: that

1. What very rare form of the verb do you see in *imponere*? Hint: It is not the infinitive!

2. Lesson 28 introduced what phenomenon associated with some compound verbs in Latin? Explain fully. Therefore what function do you see in *cervici nostrae*?

3. What time do you see *gravabit*? Give the other five times, keeping the subject the same.

4. Reverse the last line (*ipse* becomes *ipsi* and *iste* becomes *isti*).

hic tibi certa domus [est], certi (ne absiste) penates.
neu belli terrere minis; tumor omnis et irae
concessere deum.

Aeneid 8.39–41

Vocabulary: *hic*: here
absistere: to go away, stop
penates, penatium (m pl): household gods
neu: and do not
deum = *deorum*

1. What function do you identify in *tibi*? Give two possible translations for that word.

2. From the word *minae, minarum* (threats, menaces), what two possible functions could the word *minis* perform?

3. You will be more likely to pick the right one if you identify the rare form of the verb *terrere* (it's not an infinitive).

4. Look up the verbs *concesso* (I cease) and *concedo* (I withdraw). Work out what verb time you see in the form *concessere*.

"utere sorte tua. . . . Dauni miserere senectae
. . . vicisti et victum tendere palmas
Ausonii videre; tua est Lavinia coniunx,
ulterius ne tende odiis."

Aeneid 12.932

Vocabulary: *Daunus, Dauni* (m): Daunus (the speaker's father)
tendere: to stretch out and to strive, reach
Ausonii, Ausoniorum (m pl): the Italians
ulterius: farther

1. Don't be put off by the fact that the verb *utor, uti, usus sum* takes an object in the ablative function, and *misereor, misereri, miseritus sum* takes an object in the genitive function. Give the meaning of *utere* and *miserere*. Reverse each one. What is confusing about those forms at first glance?

2. What does *victum* mean on its own?

3. What two possible translations for PP2 were given as a footnote in Lesson 8?

4. And while you are there, what difficult contraction do you see in *vidēre*?

5. What mood of the verb do you see in *ne tende*? Give two alternative ways of expressing that negative command.

Post-Classical Latin Translation Practice

Liturgia Romana, Paulus VI (1897–1978 PC)

Laetare Ierusalem :
. . .
gaudete cum laetitia,
qui in tristitia fuistis.

Laetatus sum in his quae dicta sunt mihi:
in domum Domini ibimus.

"Graduale" Psalmus 121 (122)

Vocabulary: *his* (ablative): those things

1. From the verb *laetor, laetari, laetatus sum*, what part of the verb do you see in *laetare*? And *laetatus sum*?

2. Think long and hard about the main verb, and identify who is the antecedent of that *qui*.

3. What is the meaning of the preposition *cum*, and which function always follows it?

4. Say in Latin: "We will rejoice in the men who will have been seen by us."

Regina caeli, laetare, alleluia;
Quia quem meruisti portare, alleluia,
Resurrexit, sicut dixit, alleluia:
Ora pro nobis Deum, alleluia.

Vocabulary: *quia*: because

1. What mood do you spot in the verb form *ora*? Give the reverse form.

2. Again, thinking very hard about the subject of the main verb, identify the antecedent of *quem* and give the omitted Latin pronoun to express it.

Biblia Vulgata, Hieronymus (347–420 PC)

Et ecce mulier, quae habebat spiritum infirmitatis annis decem et octo et erat inclinata nec omnino poterat sursum respicere. Quam cum vidisset Iesus, vocavit et ait illi: "Mulier, dimissa es ab infirmitate tua," et imposuit illi manus; et confestim erecta est et glorificabat Deum. Respondens autem archisynagogus, indignans quia sabbato curasset Iesus, dicebat turbae: "Sex dies sunt, in quibus oportet operari; in his ergo venite et curamini et non in die sabbati."

Evangelium Secundum Lucam 13.11

Vocabulary:
annis decem et octo: for eighteen years
inclinatus -a -um: bent down
cum vidisset: when he had seen
illi: to her, upon her
erigere: to raise up
respondens / indignans (subject): replying / finding it unworthy
curasset: had cured
oportet: it is fitting
in his: during these

1. What voice, verb time and subject do you identify in *dimissa es* and *erecta est*? Give the other five times in the same voice, keeping the subject the same.

2. What two things can the passive form *curamini* be? Which will you choose here and why?

3. From the verb *operor, operari, operatus sum*, what must *operari* mean?

4. Give the reverse form of the following words: *infirmitatis, infirmitate, turbae.*

LUDUS 9

AFTER LESSONS 27–29

Topics covered: *deponent verbs; the dative case [function] for nouns, adjectives, and pronouns; the passive imperative.*

A.

In Libro XV Etymologiarum loquitur Isidorus Hispalensis (560–636 PC) "de civitatibus."

1. What kind of verb is *loquor, loqui, locutus sum*? What verb group does it belong to?

---

2. Translate the introductory sentence.

B.

De auctoribus conditarum urbium plerumque dissensio invenitur.... Primus ante diluvium Cain civitatem "Enoch" ex nomine filii sui in Naid condidit, quam urbem sola multitudine suae posteritatis implevit.

Etymologiae 15.1.1–2

Vocabulary: *plerumque* (adverb): [find in dictionary under *plerusque*]
Cain (subject), *Enoch* (object), *Naid*: indeclinable Hebrew names
multitudo, multitudinis (f): crowd, multitude
implēre: to fill up

1. What gender is *suae*? What function-case and why?

2. What meanings can you apply to *suus -a -um*? What is the rule to select the right meaning in a specific Latin sentence?

3. So what meaning must you give to *suae* and *sui* in this text and why? Why do they have the same meaning but different endings?

4. What percentage for Block 2 nouns do you notice in the form *urbium*? What is the reversed form of *conditarum urbium*?

5. From the adjective *solus -a -um* (alone, sole, one), what four possibilities exist for the form *sola*? Which function-case is it in this text? What distinguishes this function in terms of quantity, but is only readily identifiable in poetry? (Lesson 25)

6. Given the multiple meanings for some prepositions, if you don't like "out of" for *ex*, what translation will work in this text? And if you don't like "from" for *de*, what will you choose instead here?

7. From the verb *condere* (to found), what does *conditarum* mean on its own?

8. Translate the passage of Isidorus.

9. Making the necessary adaptations, transform the second sentence into your own Latin: "Before the deluge, the city Enoch was founded by Adam's [*Adamus -i* (m)] son, by whom his brother was killed, according to the famous [*clarus -a -um* AND *illustris -e*, use both] name of his son." Think carefully about the subjects before translating "his."

10. From the verb *impleo, implēre, implevi, impetum* (to fill up), give the meaning and reverse form of the following:

a. *impleveris*

b. *impleris*

c. *implere*!

d. *impleberis*

C.

Libro in operis sui quarto noster sermocinatur "de medicina" Isidorus:

Medicina est quae corporis vel tuetur vel restaurat salutem, cuius materia versatur in morbis et vulneribus. Ad hanc ita pertinent non ea tantum quae ars eorum exhibet qui proprie medici nominantur, sed etiam cibus et potus et tegumen, defensio denique omnis atque munitio qua nostrum corpus adversus externos ictus casusque servatur. (4.1.1–2)

Vocabulary:
restaurare (1): to restore
versare (1): to turn, occupy, busy
hanc (f object sing): this [*medicinam*]
pertinēre: to reach, pertain, belong
tantum: only, so much
exhibēre: to show, offer, exhibit

proprie (adverb): properly
munitio, munitionis (f): fortification, protection
servare (1): to PREserve (not serve!)

1. When you see a verb like *tueor, tueri, tuitus sum,* you know it must be translated with what kind of meaning and why?

2. What technical name is given to this kind of verb? Explain the name's derivation from Latin.

3. In the first sentence, what other indication is there of the special nature of the verb *tuetur*?

4. What could be challenging, to a reader in a hurry, about *tuetur* and *servatur*? Where do you always go to solve such problems?

5. What two meanings are possible for *eorum*? Which translation sounds best for *ars eorum . . . qui*?

6. The next lesson will give you *ictus -us* (m) (blow) and *casus -us* (m) (fall, mishap, chance). From the adjective used to describe them by Isidore, you can see that they must be which number and function?

7. Reverse the following forms from the text:

   a. *ea*

   b. *materia*

   c. *qua*

   d. *medicina*

8. Translate the whole passage.

9. Rewrite the end of the passage to produce this Latin: "protection, by which our body preserves itself and its health against their external blows."

D.

Rome's greatest author of epigrams, Marcus Valerius Martialis (40–104 PC) describes the view of Rome from Garibaldi's statue on the Janiculum Hill.

Hinc septem dominos videre montis
Et totam licet aestimare Romam,
Albanos quoque Tusculosque colles
Et quodcumque iacet sub urbe frigus.

Epigrammatum Liber 4.64.11–14

Vocabulary: [If *montis* is NOT genitive sing, then what can it be??]
licere: to be allowed
aestimare: to evaluate
quoque: also
qui-cumque, quae-cumque, quod-cumque: whatever
frigus, frigoris (n): cold, cool spot

1. From the verbs *iacio, iacere* (to throw) and *iaceo, iacēre* (to lie), give the exact meaning of *iacemus* and *iaciemus*.

2. Translate Martial's verses.

3. Add a few Latin delights and write in Latin: "To [dative] Roman parents and their children it was always allowed [Time?] to admire [*admiror* (1)] the city's beauties [*venustas, venustatis* (f)] from our hill, whose every [*omnis -e*] corner has its history [*historia -ae* (f)] and offers [*praebēre*] to its every inhabitant [*incola -ae* (c)] and his/her companion [*sodalis -is* (c)] many views [*prospectus -us* (m)] together with ice cream [*gelidus -a -um* + *sorbitio -onis* (f)]. Try it! [use *experior, experiri*, sing & pl]."

LESSON 30

THE REMAINING NOUNS IN THE DICTIONARY

Of the remaining nouns we have not yet learned (that is, nouns that are neither Block 1 nor Block 2), 10 percent are **-us -us nouns**, and are normally masculine or feminine (though there are a handful of neuters among them). Most of these endings have similarities to Block 1 or Block 2, especially if you think of them as having the key vowel "u" running through them.

fructus, fructus (m), *enjoyment, fruit, profit*

	Singular	*Plural*
Subject	**-us**	**-us**
Object	**-um**	**-us**
Genitive (of)	**-us**	**-uum**
Dative (to-for-from)	**-ui**	**-ibus**
Ablative (by-with-from-in)	**-u**	**-ibus**

The other 10 percent are **-es -ei nouns**, all of which are feminine. Most of these endings also have similarities to Block 1 and Block 2, especially if you think of them as having the key vowel "e" running through them.

species, speciei (f), *outward appearance, shape, form*

	Singular	*Plural*
Subject	-es	-es
Object	**-em**	-es
Genitive (of)	-ei	**-erum**
Dative (to-for-from)	-ei	**-ebus**
Ablative (by-with-from-in)	-e	**-ebus**

pro re publica	*for the state*
tuarum manuum opus	*the work of your hands*
defensor fidei	*defender of the faith*
meam laudat speciem	*he praises my appearance*
paucis diebus	*in a few days*

Classical Latin Translation Practice

PUBLIUS OVIDIUS NASO (43 AC–18 PC)

quo properas, ingrata viris, ingrata puellis?
roscida purpurea supprime lora manu!
Ante tuos ortus melius sua sidera servat
navita nec media nescius errat aqua;

Amores 1.13.9–12

Vocabulary: *ortus us* (m): a rising
melius (adverb): better
servare: to observe

— ⏕ | — ⏕ | — ⏕ | — ⏕ | — ⏑⏑ | — x

— ⏕ | — ⏕ | — // — ⏑⏑ | — ⏑⏑ | —

1. Try to use the scansion to solve the problem of the *a* endings in lines 1, 2, and 4. An ablative singular is long in quantity. This is just a fun challenge—scansion will be covered in the last lesson of the advanced workbook!

2. As a question word, what does *quo* mean?

3. Ovid is addressing *Aurora*. What function do you see in *viris* and *puellis*? Give the reverse of each form.

4. Reverse *tuos ortus* and *purpurea manu.*

Lucius Annaeus Seneca (4 AC–65 PC)

Excute istos qui quae cupiere deplorant et de earum rerum loquuntur fuga quibus carere non possunt.

Ad Lucilium Epistulae Morales 22

Vocabulary: *excutere*: to investigate
istos (object): those men
carere + ablative: to do without

1. Give the reverse form of *excute.*

2. Apply the relative box rule very meticulously and identify which verb must link with *quae*, and which two verbs link with *qui.*

3. With further meticulous analysis, you can provide the omitted Latin antecedent of *quae.*

4. Remind yourself of the preposition *de* (Lesson 25). Which noun has to be the object of that preposition?

5. Reverse *earum rerum.*

6. Look carefully at the information given about *carere*, and identify the function of *quibus* in its own box.

M. Cicero inter Catilinas, Clodios iactatus Pompeiosque et Crassos, partim manifestos inimicos, partim dubios amicos . . . nec secundis rebus quietus nec adversarum patiens, quotiens illum ipsum consulatum suum non sine causa sed sine fine laudatum detestatur!

De Brevitate Vitae 5.1

Vocabulary: *quietus -a -um*: quiet, peaceful
secundus -a -um: favorable
adversus -a -um: adverse
patiens, patientis: patient
illum ipsum (object): that very

1. How is Cicero described by the principal part *iactatus*?

2. He is then described by the adjectives *quietus* and *patiens*. Identify the function of *secundis rebus* and choose the best natural translation for that function which fits here.

3. What part of the word *res, rei* (f): "circumstance," is missing from the phrase *nec adversarum patiens*?

4. What is the main verb of the whole sentence? What is special about this type of verb? Explain fully. Give the other five times of that verb, keeping the subject the same.

5. What is the object of the main verb? Which four words describe it?

Post-Classical Latin Translation Practice

From the twitter feed of Papa Franciscus (b. 1936 PC)

Tuus adventus in paginam publicam Papae Francisci breviloquentis optatissimus est.

Vocabulary: *breviloquens, breviloquentis*: speaking briefly
optatissimus -a -um: very much desired

1. List all the different functions *adventus* could perform. Which will you select here?

Post tres dies, nativitas celebrabitur Domini et nos cogitamus speciali modo de familiis quae in his diebus festis iterum se coniungunt. Nativitas Domini sit pro omnibus occasio ad fraternitatem, ad augmentum in fide adque gestus solidarietatis erga omnes qui sunt in necessitate.

22 December 2019

Vocabulary: *his* (ablative): these
sit: should be
gestus -us (m): gesture, attitude

1. Which verb links with *quae*? What is the antecedent of *quae*?

2. Which verb links with *qui*? What is the antecedent of *qui*?

3. What subject, verb time, and voice do you identify in *celebrabitur*? Give the reverse form.

Tunc igitur scimus curnam, simul cum auscultatione et auditione, apud sanctum Ioannem fides sit "tangere," ut ait in Prima Epistula: "Quod audivimus, quod vidimus . . . et manus nostrae contrectaverunt de verbo vitae" (1 Io 1,1.3).

Lumen Fidei: Fides veluti auditio et visio 31

Vocabulary: *curnam* = *cur* + *nam*: why particularly
sit: is
ut: as
ait: he says

1. Look all the way back at your prepositions followed by the object function (Lesson 6) and select a meaning for *apud* that works well here.

2. Look at the footnote to the second table in Lesson 8, remind yourself which two translations are possible for PP2, and apply this to *tangere*.

3. Reverse the last six words.

Peramplus exstat consensus scientificus qui indicat quandam inesse calefactionem systematis climatici quae sollicitudinem concitat. Postremis decenniis eiusmodi calefactio constanti ducta est augmento gradus maris, quod praeterea facile coniungitur cum augmento eventuum meteorologicorum extremorum, quamvis causa ex scientia determinabilis unicuique eventui non sit singillatim adscribenda.

Laudato si': Clima velute commune bonum 23

Vocabulary: *quandam* (object): a certain
inesse: to be present
postremus -a -um: the most recent
decennium -ii (n): decade
eiusmodi: of this kind
constans, constantis: constant
ducere: to calculate, deduce, accompany
gradus, gradus (m): level, step
facile: easily
unicuique (dative): for each
non sit singillatim adscribenda: is not to be individually assigned

1. What are the respective antecedents of *qui*, *quae*, and *quod* in the text above? Carefully connect the correct verb with each relative pronoun.

2. What is the feminine subject of *ducta est*?

3. With what noun does the adjective *constanti* agree?

4. Give the reverse forms of *eventuum* and *eventui*.

LESSON 31

COMMON CONTRACTIONS OF VERB FORMS; A NOTE ON THE REMAINING IRREGULAR VERBS

Contractions

Swallowed "V" in Times 4-5-6

Many contractions occur because the letter "v" was pronounced with a weak "u" sound. This "u" sound, combined with a vowel, is easy to swallow up when you are pronouncing a word quickly. Hence:

puta(vi)sti	*you thought*	becomes **putasti**
no(vi)sti	*you have got to know*	becomes **nosti**
puta(ve)rant	*they had thought*	becomes **putarant**
no(ve)ram	*I had got to know*	becomes **noram**
puta(ve)rint	*They will have thought*	becomes **putarint**
no(ve)ro	*I will have got to know*	becomes **noro**

These are common, for example, in Cicero's informal letters, where their use reflects real Roman street talk.

T.4 *erunt* Becomes *ēre*

This contraction is very common in both poetry and prose. Stay on your toes and look at the stem. The contracted T.4 will have PP3 as the stem, and mostly differ from PP2.

fulserunt	*they shone*	becomes **fulsēre**

Ris to *Re* in Times 1-2-3 Passive

The *tu* passive form for Times 1-2-3 is often contracted from *ris* to *re*

amaberis	*you will be loved*	may be written **amabere**
amabaris	*you were being loved*	may be written **amabare**
amaris	*you are loved*	may be written **amare**

Obviously these contractions produce all sorts of fun and games: ... is *amare* PP2? Is it the passive imperative? Is it an adverb meaning "bitterly"? Is it Time 1 passive? What is *amavere*?

"Homines," inquit, "emisti, coegisti, parasti."

Cicero, *Pro Sestio*

---

contentus niveis semper vectabere cycnis,
nec te fortis equi ducet ad arma sonus.

Propertius, *Elegiae* 3.3

Five More Irregular Verbs

All verbs are regular in Times 4-5-6.

eo, ire, i(v)i, itum: *go*

compounds: **pereo, adeo, redeo, exeo, intereo, &c**
T.1: *eo, is, it, imus, itis, eunt*
T.2: *ibam, ibas,* &c
T.3: *ibo, ibis,* &c

volo, velle, volui: *want, wish*

T.1: *volo, vis, vult, vultis, volumus, volunt*
T.2: *volebam, volebas,* &c
T.3: *volam, voles,* &c

nolo, nolle, nolui: *not want, refuse*

T.1: *nolo, non vis, non vult, nolumus, non vultis, nolunt*
T.2: *nolebam, nolebas,* &c
T.3: *nolam, noles,* &c

malo, malle, malui: *prefer*

T.1: *malo, mavis, mavult, malumus, mavultis, malunt*
T.2: *malebam, malebas,* &c
T.3: *malam, males,* &c

fero, ferre, tuli, latus: *bring, carry, bear*

compounds: **refero, confero**
T.1: *fero, fers, fert, ferimus, fertis, ferunt*
T.2: *ferebam, ferebas,* &c
T.3: *feram, feres,* &c
imperative: *fer, ferte*

Laudes vultis dicere Deo? (Augustinus)

CELEBRATORY LUDUS 10

AFTER LESSONS 30–31

Topics covered: -us -us *and* -es -ies *nouns; verb contractions; irregular verbs.*

The most celebrated relationship-romance-drama of the Middle Ages was that between teacher, philosopher, and theologian Petrus Abelardus (1079–1142 PC) and the student-wife-cloistered nun and abbess Heloisa; it was immortalized in their love letters. Here are some texts of a letter from her to him. She was highly educated!

A.

She speaks of her retreat into the monastery on his advice, to dissipate the scandal:

> **[me] quidem iuvenculam ad monasticae conversionis asperitatem non religionis devotio sed tua tantum pertraxit iussio . . . / . . . properantem te ad deum secuta sum habitu, immo praecessi. quasi enim memor uxoris Loth retro conversae prius me sacris vestibus et professione monastica quam te ipsum Deo mancipasti . . . / . . . non enim mecum animus meus sed tecum erat. sed nunc maxime si tecum non est, nusquam est. esse vero sine te nequaquam potest.**
>
> *Epistula* II

Vocabulary: *tantum*: only
pertrahere: to drag, draw
properans, properantis: hurrying, rushing
habitus -us (m): habit, religious clothing
immo: nay rather
praecedere: to go ahead, precede

quasi: as if, like, just as
Loth: of Lot
convertere: to turn around
prius . . . quam . . . : sooner . . . than . . .
te ipsum (object): you yourself
mancipo (1): deliver, hand over, sell
maxime: mostly
vero: in fact, however

1. You can immediately spot the time of the verb *mancipasti* and reverse that form. How would you write that contracted verb out in full?

2. In line 1, which noun is the object of the preposition *ad*?

3. What is the reversed form for the *te* in line 2? Explain your answer fully. What is the reversed form of the *te* in the last line? Explain fully.

4. Using your dictionary, you can identify the function-case of *memor*. Whom is it describing here?

5. From the clues in the sentence or other methods, how do you know that *secuta sum* is a deponent verb? Check the dictionary and state the group to which the verb belongs. Give the other five verb times in Latin and English, keeping the subject the same.

6. How does the story change if you read *secutus sum*?

7. What two possible functions-cases can *sacris vestibus* be? Give the reverse form for each case. What case will you choose for your translation and why?

8. What function-case is *habitu*? For that same noun, list all the possible functions that the word *habitus* can have.

9. Now give your own polished translation of the whole passage.

10. Say in Latin:

a. "Peter and Heloissa expressed their love between themselves by their lovey-dovey [*amatorius -a -um*] writings [PP4 of *scribo*...]."

b. "The love of Peter and Heloissa between them was expressed by their every lovey-dovey writing."

B.

She testifies to the extent of her feelings towards him. (Measure your progress since Lesson 8!)

in tantam versus est amor insaniam ... ut te tam corporis mei quam animi unicum possessorem ostenderem. nihil umquam—Deus scit—in te nisi te requisivi, te pure non tua concupiscens. non matrimonii foedera non dotes aliquas exspectavi, non denique meas voluptates aut voluntates sed tuas—sicut ipse nosti—adimplere studui.

Epistula II

Vocabulary:
vertere: to turn, convert
ut: that
tam ... quam ... : as much ... as ...
nisi: if not, unless, except
pure: purely, solely
concupiscens, concupiscentis: desiring
foedus, foederis (n): pact, contract
dos, dotis (f): dowry
aliquas (f object pl): some, any
denique: finally
adimplere: to fulfil

1. What does *tua* mean on its own?

2. Give the reverse forms for the three instances of *te* in the second sentence.

3. Which noun is the object of the first word *in*?

4. How would you write *nosti* in full?

5. Now translate the whole passage, taking *ostenderem* as *ostendebam*.

Finally we come full circle, returning to the Father of Latinity, Marcus Tullius Cicero, who appeared on the first Ludus, for our final readings—one addressing the hated enemy of the state, Catiline, the other taken from Cicero's beautiful dialogue "On Friendship" (a tribute to his best friend Atticus).

C.

"refer" inquis "ad senatum."... non referam, id quod abhorret a meis moribus, et tamen faciam ut intellegas quid hi de te sentiant. egredere ex urbe, Catilina, libera rem publicam metu, in exsilium, si hanc vocem exspectas, proficiscere.

Oratio Prima in Catiliinam 1.20.8

Vocabulary: *abhorrere*: to differ, shrink
faciam ut: I shall see to it that
intellegas and *sentiant*: [translate as T.1]
hi (subject pl): these men
res publica: the state, the republic
hanc (f object sing): this

1. What mood / time of the irregular verb *referre* (to bring a motion) do you see in the forms *refer* and *referam*? Give the six times for *referam*, with "he" as the subject.

2. What mood do you see in the words *egredere*, *libera*, and *proficiscere*? Reverse each one. Why do they not look the same?

3. Translate the passage from this very famous speech.

D.

ex omnibus rebus, quas mihi aut fortuna aut natura tribuit, nihil habeo, quod cum amicitia Scipionis possim comparare. In hac mihi de re publica consensus, in hac rerum privatarum consilium, in eadem requies plena oblectationis fuit.

Laelius de Amicitia 103

Vocabulary: *aut ... aut ...* : either ... or ...
tribuere: to grant, give
Scipio, Scipionis (m): Publius Cornelius Scipio Aemilianus Africanus Minor (185/4–129 AC)
possim: I could
in hac [amicitia]: in this friendship
consilium -i (n): counsel, considering together

1. Give seven possible translations for the verb *tribuit*.

2. Translate the passage.

3. Say in Latin: "From each thing, which the readings [*lectio*] have given to us, there is nothing as full of delights as [*tam ... quam ...*] the wisdom [*sapientia*] of Cicero."

REFERENCE MATERIALS

Reference Sheet 1: A Concordance/Glossary of Terminology

Fr. Reginald Foster	*Traditional*
Block 1	first and second declension
Block 2	third declension
-us -us nouns	fourth declension
-es -ei nouns	fifth declension
relative box / language capsule	subordinate clause
Time 1	the present tense
Time 2	the imperfect tense
Time 3	the future tense
Time 4a and 4b	the perfect tense
Time 5	the pluperfect tense
Time 6	the future perfect tense
function	case
subject	nominative
object	accusative
of-possession	genitive
by-with-from-in	ablative
to-for-from	dative
masculine / feminine / neuter	gender
number	singular or plural
reverse	give the opposite form (singular to plural or vice versa)
fence verbs	mixed conjugation verbs
verb groups	conjugations
flip	exchange active person endings for passive person endings (or vice versa)

Reference Sheet 2: The Importance of the Dictionary

If you could swallow Lewis and Short or the *Oxford Latin Dictionary* (*OLD*) you would know the language. The dictionary is your bible, so you need to trust it and use the information it is giving you. Anything odd about a word, in form or use, will be in the dictionary.

Add to these lists as you read, *and in your own terms*, but here is some basic information about words as they appear in the dictionary:

Nouns

Nouns appear in the dictionary with two word forms (subject singular and of-possession [genitive] singular) and the gender (m/f/n).

-is in the genitive singular is the sign of Block 2

servus -i **(m)**; *puellae -ae* **(f)**; *templum -i* **(n)**; *leo, leonis* **(m)**; *exercitus, exercitus* **(m)**

Verbs

Verbs appear in the dictionary with up to four principal parts (PPs). Any strangeness in or absence of PP will be indicated. The PPs always give the same information.

- PP1—*ego* Time 1
- PP2—the contemporaneous infinitive / gerund
- PP3—*ego* Time 4
- PP4—passive past participle ("having been . . .")
- The PP1 of a deponent verb (still *ego* T.1) ends in *-or.*
- You can tell the group of a verb from the appearance of its PPs, but the dictionary might also give you the group number in brackets. The dictionary will also tell you how the verb is used—what constructions ("with *ut*: . . .") or special function-cases follow it ("with *dat.*: . . ."); it will tell you whether the verb is transitive, and takes a direct object ("v. a."), or is intransitive, and doesn't ("v. n.").

sequor, sequi, secutus sum

odi, odisse

amo (1)

Adjectives & Pronouns

Adjectives and pronouns normally appear in the dictionary with three word forms (m / f / n subject singular). Where two parts are given, the first part is the masculine and feminine (which are the same for that word), and the neuter subject singular.

celer, celeris, celere

bonus, bona, bonum

ille, illa, illud

qui, quae, quod

quis, quid

Words with Block 1 and 2 endings, together with the endings, are given on Reference Sheets 4 and 5.

Reference Sheet 2: Word Clouds: Make Your Own

- You will get so used to word types that gradually you will be able to reconstruct the dictionary entry from the word you are reading in a passage. **Practice, practice: all is coming.**
- Understanding the dictionary gives you the word type and block/group and therefore what endings it will have.

Some Verbs for "Go" and Their Compounds

-gredior, -gredi, -gressus sum	**accedo**
aggredior	**incedo**
egredior	**procedo**
ingredior	**recedo**
progredior	
regredior	

- You can make similar lists for the compounds of *facio* and *fero*.

-as, -atis (f)—Many Feminine Abstract Nouns

aetas, aetatis (f); dignitas, dignitatis (f); veritas, veritatis (f)

Reference Sheet 3: Translation Toolkit

quae nimium vorax erat olim dea suum iussit amicum tria poma sui patrui ex horto sibi ferre, quamquam hoc difficile erat quod ferox poma semper canis servabat.

Vocabulary: *vorax, voracis*: greedy, voracious, destructive
pomum, pomi (n): apple
patruus, patrui (m): uncle
difficilis, difficile: difficult

1. Read the whole sentence to the full-stop. Remember the word order in Latin will **not** be the same as your English version.
2. Check if there are any relative boxes or language capsules (subordinate clauses). These are introduced by *qui*, *quae*, *quod*, *cum*, *ubi*, *postquam*, *quamquam*, *ut*, *ne*, &c. Mark this box with brackets. The first verb that follows one of these words **must** go with it. **Do not translate this verb first.** It is not the main verb.
3. Find the main verb.
4. Work out the time of the main verb.
5. Work out who or what is doing the main verb.
6. See if there is a noun, an adjective on its own, or a pronoun in the sentence that could be doing that verb (look for subject [*nominative*] endings).
7. Do any adjectives agree with that noun (subject [*nominative*] endings)?
8. Find any direct objects of the verb (look for object [*accusative*] endings). Do any adjectives agree with that direct object (adjectives with object [*accusative*] endings)?
9. Translate any adverbs.
10. Translate any prepositional phrases. Remember, prepositions are followed by object (*accusative* or *ablative*) endings. Do any adjectives describe the noun governed by the preposition?
11. Analyze any words you have left: What type of word is it? If it is a noun, pronoun, or adjective, work out what function (case) it is. Otherwise look out for clues. For example, if the

main verb is "I want" or "I am able," it is likely that there will be an infinitive somewhere in the sentence. If the verb is "I give" or "I bring," it is likely there is a *dative*.

12. Once you have dealt with the main sentence go back and repeat steps 4 through 11 for the relative box or language capsule, this time not for the main verb but for the verb in the subordinate clause.

Reference Sheet 4: Block 1 and Types of Words with These Endings

	Singular			*Plural*		
	M	*F*	*N*	*M*	*F*	*N*
Subject	-us	-a	-um	-i	-ae	-a
Object	-um	-am	-um	-os	-as	-a
Genitive (of)	-i	-ae	-i	-orum	-arum	-orum
Dative (to-for-from)	-o	-ae	-o	-is	-is	-is
Ablative (by-with-from-in)	-o	-a	-o	-is	-is	-is
Vocative	-e	-a	-um	-i	-ae	-a

All the following types of words have Block 1 endings:

Block 1 Nouns: subject singular, genitive singular (gender)

captivus, captivi (m): *prisoner*
ager, agri (m): *field*
puella, puellae (f): *girl*
verbum, verbi (n): *word*

Block 1 Adjectives: masculine subject singular, f subj sing, n subj sing

bonus, bona, bonum: *good*
miser, misera, miserum: *miserable*

Passive Past Participle: PP4 of Normal Verbs

The verb "to lead"

duco, ducere, duxi, ductus -a -um

gives the participle

ductus, ducta, ductum: *having been led*

Active Past Participle: PP3 of Deponent Verbs (without the *sum*!)

The verb "to set out":

egredior, egredi, egressus

gives the participle

egressus, egressa, egressum: *having set out*

Pronouns in Latin (More detail in the intermediate workbook)

Loosely speaking, most pronouns in Latin have endings rather like Block 1 (**with the exception that genitive singular is -*ius* and dative singular is -*i***). Using this as a starting point will help you figure out their function, gender, and number.

is, ea, id:	*he/she/it*
qui, quae, quod:	*who, which*
hic, haec, hoc:	*this*
ille, illa, illud:	*that*
iste, ista, istud:	*that*

*Exception: the dative and ablative plural of *qui, quae, quod*: who/which, is **quibus**; neuter subject and object plural of *hic, haec, hoc* is **haec**.

The Special Nine

The special nine share the exception that genitive singular is *ius* and dative singular is *i.*

Unus -a -um	*one or only*
Nullus -a -um	*none, no*
Ullus -a -um	*any, some*
Solus -a -um	*only, sole*
Neuter, neutra, neutrum	*neither* **(of two)**
Alter, altera, alterum	*the other* **(of two, i.e., not** *another*)
Uter, utra, utrum (uterque)	*each* **(of two) (NB: utrum** = *whether*)
Totus, tota, totum	*the whole, entire* **(not** *all*)
Alius, alia, aliud	*other or another* **(of many)**

Self-Same-Certain

ipse, ipsa, ipsum:	*the very, self*
idem, eadem, idem:	*the same*
quidam, quaedam, quoddam:	*a certain*

Reference Sheet 5: Block 2 and Types of Words with These Endings

	Singular		*Plural*	
	M/F	*N*	*M/F*	*N*
Subject	[crazy]	[crazy]	**-es**	**-a / -ia** [80/20 rule]
Object	**-em**	[crazy]	**-es**	**-a / -ia** [80/20 rule]
Genitive (of)	**-is**	**-is**	**-um / -ium** [80/20 rule]	**-um / -ium** [80/20 rule]
Dative (to-for-from)	**-i**	**-i**	**-ibus**	**-ibus**
Ablative (by-with-from-in)	**-e / -i** [80/20 rule]	**-e / -i** [80/20 rule]	**-ibus**	**-ibus**
Vocative	[crazy]	[crazy]	**-es**	**-a / -ia** [80/20 rule]

Block 2 Nouns & Adjectives: subject singular, genitive singular (gender)

vox, vocis (f): *voice*

ferox, ferocis: *fierce*

Block 2 Adjectives: m/f subj sing, n subj sing

omnis, omne: *all, every*

Block 2 Adjectives: m subject singular, f subj sing, n subj sing

celer, celeris, celere: *quick, fast*

Reference Sheet 6: Regular Verb Cheat Sheet

Which group does the verb belong to?			*The meaning of the 4 principal parts*	
PP1	*PP2*	*Group*	*PP1*	*PP2*
-o	-are	1 (a)	**canto** ego time 1	**cantare** infinitive
-eo	-ere	2 (e)		
-o	-ere	3 (e)	I sing	to sing (singing)
			Deponent verbs	
-io	-ire	4 (i)		
-io	-ere	fence (i)	**conor**	**conari**
sum	**esse**	irregular	**sequor**	**sequi**

Times 1-2-3 Active: USE PP1	*Times 1-2-3 ACTIVE*	
Time 1: theme vowel of group + person endings. Exception: Group 3 use **i**; Group 3/4/fence, they = **-unt**	**1 present**	It sings It is singing
Time 2: see **-ba** + person endings	**2 imperfect**	It was singing It used to sing
Time 3: Groups 1 & 2 add **-bo, -bis, -bit, -bimus, -bitis, -bunt**; Groups 3/4/fence add **-am, -es, -et, -emus, -etis, -ent**	**3 future**	It will sing

Times 4-5-6 Active: USE PP3	*Times 4-5-6 ACTIVE*	
Time 4: keep **PP3** and add Time 4 special** endings	**4 perfect**	It has sung It sang
Time 5: PP3 without the i, add **-eram, -eras, -erat, -eramus, -eratis, -erant**	**5 pluperfect**	It had sung
Time 6: PP3 without the i, add **-ero, -eris -erit, -erimus, -eritis, -erint**	**6 future perfect**	It will have sung

IMPERATIVES	**1 – are**	**2 – ēre**
tu – vos A	**ama – amate**	**habe – habete**
tu – vos – ii B	**amato – amatote – amanto!**	

The meaning of the 4 principal parts

PP3	PP4
cantavi	**cantatus -a -um**
ego time 4	passive past participle
I have sung I sang	having been sung

Deponent verbs

conatus sum **secutus sum**	X

The ending on the verb tells you who is doing the verb

Person	*Ending*	Time 4**
I	-o/-m	*-i*
you	-s	*-sti*
he/she/it	-t	*-t*
we	-mus	*-mus*
you plural	-tis	*-stis*
they	-nt	*-erunt*

Times 1-2-3 PASSIVE

1 present	It is sung It is being sung
2 imperfect	It was being sung It kept being sung
3 future	It will be sung

Times 1-2-3 Passive: USE PP1

As for Active 1-2-3, then flip the ending to passive. NB—'-iris'mostly changes to '-eris'

I	-or/-r
you	-ris
he/she/it	-tur
we	-mur
you plural	-mini
they	-ntur

Times 4-5-6 PASSIVE

4 perfect	It has been sung It was sung
5 pluperfect	It had been sung
6 future perfect	It will have been sung

Times 4-5-6 Passive: USE PP4

Time 4: PP4 (must agree with subject) + *Time 1 of "sum, esse, fui"*: **sum, es, est, sumus, estis, sunt**

Time 5: PP4 (must agree with subject) + *Time 2 of "sum, esse, fui"*: **eram, eras, erat, eramus, eratis, erant**

Time 6: PP4 (must agree with subject) + *Time 3 of "sum, esse, fui"*: **ero, eris, erit, erimus, eritis, erunt**

3 & fence – ere	*4 – ire*
scribe – scribite	**audi – audite**
audito – auditote – audiunto!	

Passive imperative

tu: "active" infinitive: **sequere!**

vos: T.1: **sequimini!**

FINIS

INDEX OF TRANSLATIONS BY AUTHOR OR WORK

INDEX OF LESSONS

Ossa Ostensa: A Proven System for Demystifying Latin was
designed in Minion with Meta Sans display type and composed
by Kachergis Book Design of Pittsboro, North Carolina. It was printed on
60-pound White Offset and bound by Data Reproductions,
Auburn Hills, Michigan.